HOTSPOTS
ALGA

Written by Chris and Melanie Rice, updated by Barbara Rogers
Front cover photography courtesy of Thomas Cook Tour Operations Ltd

Original concept by Studio 183 Limited
Series design by Bridgewater Books
Cover design/artwork by Lee Biggadike, Studio 183 Limited

Produced by the Bridgewater Book Company
The Old Candlemakers, West Street, Lewes, East Sussex BN7 2NZ, United Kingdom
www.bridgewaterbooks.co.uk
Project Editor: Emily Casey Bailey
Project Designer: Lisa McCormick

Published by Thomas Cook Publishing
A division of Thomas Cook Tour Operations Limited
PO Box 227, Units 15-16, Coningsby Road, Peterborough PE3 8SB, United Kingdom
email: books@thomascook.com
www.thomascookpublishing.com
+ 44 (0) 1733 416477

ISBN-13: 978-1-84157-520-9
ISBN-10: 1-84157-520-8

First edition © 2006 Thomas Cook Publishing
Text © 2006 Thomas Cook Publishing
Maps © 2006 Thomas Cook Publishing
Head of Thomas Cook Publishing: Chris Young
Project Editor: Diane Ashmore
Production/DTP Editor: Steven Collins

Printed and bound in Spain by Graficas Cems, Navarra, Spain

CONTENTS

SYMBOLS KEY

The following is a key to the symbols used throughout this book:

i	information office	**✝**	church	🛍	shopping
P	car park		train station	🍴	restaurant
🚌	bus stop	🛡	police station	☕	café
☎	telephone	✈	airport	🍸	bar
✉	post office	↘	tip	☖	fine dining

☎ telephone	**f** fax	**e** email	**w** website address
a address	🕐 opening times	**!** important	

€ budget price €€ mid-range price €€€ most expensive

★ specialist interest ★★ see if passing ★★★ top attraction

INTRODUCTION
Getting to know the Algarve

ODECEIXE

MONTE CLERIGO
ALJEZUR
VALE DA TELHA

S. MARCOS
DA SERRA

MONCHIQUE

CASAIS

S. BAR
DE ME

BORDEIRA

ALCALAR

SILVES

BANSAFRIM

ALGOZ

ODIÁXERE
ALVOR
PORTIMÃO

PRAIA
DE LUZ
LAGOS
PRAIA DA
ROCHA
LAGOA

VILA DO BISPO
FERRAGUDO
ARMAÇÃO
DE PÊRA
ALBUFE

BURGAU
CARVOEIRO
GALE

SALEMA

Cape
St Vincent

SAGRES

MONTECHIQUE

ATLANTIC OCEAN

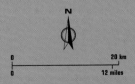

N

| 0 | | 20 km |
| 0 | | 12 miles |

Getting to know the Algarve

More than two million European visitors head for the Algarve every year. Why do they come? For most people the climate and the beaches are the main attractions. The Algarve basks in more than 3000 hours of sunshine per year; the winters are mild, the summers long and hot. Even in the coolest months temperatures rarely fall below 15°C (59°F), while in July and August 29°C (84°F) is the norm. In the eastern Algarve, the long, unbroken expanses of golden sand are ideal for swimming and sunbathing. In the west lies a succession of bays, inlets and rocky coves, sheltered by dramatic sandstone cliffs, creating magical places to laze the day away.

Those looking for a more active holiday will appreciate the first-class sporting facilities, including no fewer than 16 golf courses, designed to show off the beauties of the countryside as well as test the skills of the players. Besides golf, there are opportunities for deep-sea fishing, windsurfing, horse riding, sailing, lawn bowling and tennis. And for walkers, there are plenty of dunes and cliff paths that are perfect for a gentle ramble with outstanding views.

The Algarve offers just as much variety in its nightlife. You can dine out at a romantic cliff-top restaurant, on a terrace overlooking the beach or in a converted fisherman's cottage; stop for a sundowner in a cocktail bar on the promenade, or enjoy a pint of beer in an English-style pub. For a touch of local colour, sign up for a *fado* evening (see below) or village-restaurant barbecue. Then dance the night away in a disco or nightclub, or, if you are feeling lucky, have a flutter in one of the casinos.

WHAT IS *FADO*?

Fado music is as important to the Portuguese as *flamenco* is to the Spanish. *Fado* ballads are plaintive and dramatic, usually about lost or unrequited love and the ups-and-downs of life. The singer, or *fadista*, traditionally wears black to commemorate Maria Severa, a famous 19th-century performer who died tragically young. The accompaniment is provided by two guitarists.

⬤ *Praia d'Alvor, a typical Algarvian cove*

THE PORTUGUESE EXPERIENCE

Algarvians are a welcoming and hospitable people. Go along to a *baile*, a riotous village knees-up usually involving the entire community. The energetic dancing is accompanied by accordions, fiddles, triangles and side drums, sometimes even bagpipes. You will find the uninhibited Algarvian sense of fun and enjoyment infectious. Spend time away from the beach resorts to savour the real flavour of Portugal.

AZULEJO TILES

Glazed, multicoloured *azulejo* tiles began appearing in the Algarve more than 500 years ago and are now used to decorate everything from park benches to house fronts, restaurants and even train stations. The oldest examples are in churches and chapels, where the predominantly blue tiles usually depict scenes from the bible.

The best of the Algarve

ACTIVITIES
- Enjoy the challenges of 16 golf courses (pages 14, 20, 29, 34, 41 and 50).
- Explore the unusual rock formations of the west coast.
- Scuba dive in clear water off **Ponta da Piedade** (pages 66 and 106).
- Try your hand at big-game fishing (page 105).
- Learn to windsurf at **Praia da Rocha**, or hit the west coast for big waves.
- Enjoy the countryside from horseback (page 105).

ART & HISTORY
- The ruins of a Roman villa in Milreu (page 79).
- The lavish carved interior of **Santo António** (page 66) in Lagos.
- The tiled **Capela São Lourenço dos Matos** (page 49) in Almancil.
- The Moorish castle at **Silves** (page 74), ancient capital of the Algarve.
- Medieval battlements at **Loulé** (page 88).

BEST BEACHES
- Longest: **Praia da Falésia** (page 56), **Armação de Pêra** (page 28), **Quarteira** (page 44) and **Monte Gordo** (page 52). Widest: **Praia da Rocha** (page 24).
- Windsurfing: **Meia Praia** (page 102) and **Praia do Martinhal** (page 62).
- Snorkelling and diving: **Praia da Luz** (page 16) and **Baleeira** (page 62).

EATING & DRINKING
- Take a picnic to the 'end of the world' at **Cape St Vincent** (page 60).
- Sip a sundowner on a terrace at **Praia da Rocha** (page 24).
- Take a boat trip along the coast for a beach-barbecue lunch.
- Dine in the sophisticated surroundings of **Vilamoura** marina (page 40).

EXCURSIONS
- Visit the capital **Lisbon**, and see a different face of Portugal (page 84).
- Take a jeep safari into the mountains at **Monchique** (page 68) or the **Costa Vicentina** (page 63).
- Explore the **Ria Formosa** nature reserve by bike or boat (page 81).

RESORTS
Places under the sun

Salema & Burgau
small is beautiful

Typical red-roofed fishermen's houses, a small sandy beach and cobbled streets rising gently up sandstone cliffs, characterize both the villages of Salema (pronounced 'Sah-lay-mah') and Burgau (pronounced 'Bur-gow'). With just a handful of shops, bars and restaurants, holidaymakers come here to enjoy the peace and quiet as well as the stunning scenery of the western Algarve.

Life in these tiny communities revolves around the harbours, where the local fishermen mend their nets and wash out the squid pots. Boat trips head along the coast from Salema harbour to the rocky crevices of **Ponta da Piedade** where egrets nest or, in the opposite direction, where swimmers can enjoy a dip before sitting down to a barbecue on a secluded beach. The beauty of the area can also be appreciated on foot by following the two-hour switchback walk over the headlands between Burgau and Salema, which takes in the remote coves of **Ponta da Almadena** and **Boca do Rio**.

Wake up in time to watch the sun rising over the bay and you will see the fishermen hauling in the first catch of the day; alternatively, you can enjoy their harvest at lunchtime by sampling grilled sardines in a harbour restaurant.

THINGS TO SEE & DO
Birdwatching ★
Full- and half-day trips, led by an expert, can be booked through the tourist offices at Portimão (☎ 282 41 65 56) and Lagos (☎ 282 76 30 31).

Burgau Sports Centre ★
The facilities here include a gym, football, basketball, tennis and squash courts, swimming pool and aerobics sessions, plus a children's playground and children's sports mornings. ☎ 282 69 73 50

SHOPPING

 There is a newsagent, a supermarket and a souvenir shop on Rua 25 de Abril in Burgau.

Salema has a couple of supermarkets as well as handicraft and souvenir shops on the waterfront. At **Loja do Tosca** you will find top-quality one-off designer Portuguese and ethnic clothing and accessories (beautiful belts and shoes). Sculptures are also for sale.

ⓐ Rua dos Pescadores, Salema ⏰ Open 09.00–late

The nearest banks and pharmacies are in Praia da Luz. For more comprehensive shopping, head for Lagos.

⬤ Salema's beach

Parque da Floresta Golf and Leisure Resort ★★
The excellent Parque da Floresta club offers lawn bowling (Open 10.00–dusk, competitions Mon), an 18-hole golf course plus golf academy, four tennis courts, a fitness and leisure centre, mountain-bike rental, archery (with cheap 'have-a-go sessions' Open Sat–Wed 13.00–17.00) and walking tours Vale do Poço, Budens 282 69 00 00 www.parquedafloresta.com

RESTAURANTS & BARS
Salema:

A Boia Restaurant Bar €€ Sip cocktails, enjoy fresh fish and take in the sea views. Rua dos Pescadores Open 10.00–22.00 for meals, bar until 02.00

O Carapau Francês €–€€ Attractive, informal restaurant-café for pizza, fish and meat dishes. Eat on the pretty terrace or in the tiled interior. Main square 282 69 52 53 Open 09.00–late

Mira Mar €€ Good food is available all day at reasonable prices in this typical Algarvian restaurant. The grilled swordfish is recommended. Praia da Salema 282 65 72 50 Open 09.00–late

Restaurante Atlantico €€ A beach restaurant with an extensive fish menu, including clams, tuna and *cataplana* (fish stew, see page 93). Praia da Salema 282 79 20 86 Open 10.00–late

Restaurant Florestal €€–€€€ Set among pines and eucalyptus trees, this friendly place offers an international menu. Barão de São João 282 68 72 04 Open for lunch noon–14.00, snacks 14.00–19.00, dinner 19.00–22.00, closed Nov–Apr and every Tues

A Tabua Cocktail Bar €€ The place to be seen in Salema with a cocktail, sangría, or English, German or Portuguese beer in hand. Rua dos Pescadores Open 20.30–02.00

Burgau:

 Ancora €€–€€€ Bookings are essential at this smart eatery. Vegetarian meals are available with 24 hours' notice. ❸ Largo dos Pescadores ❶ 282 69 71 02 ❶ Open 19.00–23.00, closed Mon (summer), closed Mon and Tues (low season), closed Nov–Mar

Beach Bar €€ Not only the perfect location, sitting on a raised terrace above Burgau beach, but good food – from full meals (lobster salad and T-bone steaks are the specialities) to a burger – with friendly, laid-back service. ❸ Main beach ❶ 282 69 75 53 ❶ Open 09.30–02.00, restaurant open noon–15.00 and 19.00–22.00

Caravela €€–€€€ Portuguese cuisine is served under palm trees in the garden of this charming restaurant. Try the saddle of lamb, hunter-style stewed rabbit or turbot in breadcrumbs. ❸ Rua Valedo ❶ 282 69 72 74 ❶ Open 18.30–22.30.

Casa Grande €€€ *One Foot in the Algarve* was filmed in this charming old manor house, and its former winery is now a restaurant serving up a varied menu that alternates daily between Portuguese and Indonesian, with a good choice for vegetarians. Occasional live music and folk dancing. ❸ Road to Praia da Luz ❶ 282 69 74 16 ❶ Open Mon–Fri 19.00–midnight (Mar– Nov), closed weekends and Dec–Feb

Dom Dinis €€ Set in a very peaceful location, this is a long-established traditional, rustic international/Portuguese restaurant. ❸ 1 km (0.6 miles) from Burgau on the Salema road near a bus stop ❶ 282 69 74 61 ❶ Open 10.00–15.00 and 18.30–22.30 (bar until 02.00)

Rios Negros €€ Fish (caught daily by the owner-chef) and meat dishes grilled on an open fire are served up in this popular, cosy restaurant. Jazz and popular music. ❸ Largo do Poço 4 (EN 125 between Burgau and Budens) ❶ 282 69 53 30 ❶ Open 19.30–23.00

○ *The sheltered Luz harbour*

Praia da Luz
rock slabs and sand

Whitewashed villas and holiday apartments cloaked in bougainvillaea
blend harmoniously with the picturesque old houses that cluster
round the fishing harbour of Luz (pronounced 'Loosh'). The beach
of soft sand is edged by great slabs of flat smooth rocks, which
make perfect sunbathing beds for visitors who prefer not to get
sand between their toes. The sheltered waters of the bay are ideal
for water skiing, windsurfing, sailing and diving. Luz has its own local
shops, a sprinkling of bars and restaurants and even a discotheque
near the waterfront.

SHOPPING

 The **Centro Commercial** on the seafront has a number of
outlets selling clothes, food, magazines and groceries.
Baptista's supermarket is in the centre of the village. Situated
below the Dolphin restaurant (see page 18) is the colourful **Africa
Craft Shop**, specializing in curios and handicrafts from southern
Africa. ✆ Rua da Calheta ⏱ Open 14.00–21.00

Luz's attractive hinterland is ideal for walks and drives. Take the path from the car park at the eastern end of the village to the top of the headland, where an *atalaia* (obelisk) stands at a height of 108 m (360 ft) above sea level. From here there are coastal views as far as Sagres.

The gently rolling hills to the north of Luz are best explored by car. The road winds through a landscape dotted with farms, ancient wells, fig trees and quaint villages like Barão de São João.

THINGS TO SEE & DO
Fortaleza da Luz ★
Luz's 16th-century fortress has been beautifully restored to house a fine restaurant (see page 19). Even if you don't intend eating here, don't be shy to ask to look in.

Horse riding ★
Tiffany's Riding Centre caters for young and old, novices and experts alike, and offers rides lasting from one hour to a whole holiday course. ⓐ Vale Grifo, Almádena ⓘ 282 69 73 95 ⓛ Open daily

Parish church ★
Picturesquely situated near the waterfront of the old village is the parish church, with medieval vaults and a gilded baroque altar.

Sea Sports Centre ★
This licenced diving school rents out equipment and offers lessons for all levels. ⓐ Avenida dos Pescadores, Loja 4 ⓘ 282 78 95 38

Sports ★
Facilities at the **Luz Bay** and **Ocean** clubs include swimming pools, saunas, a Turkish bath, gym, mini-golf, tennis and squash courts.

Watersports School ★
Windsurfing, sailing and water skiing are all available. ⓐ Praia da Luz ⓘ 282 77 85 81

17

RESTAURANTS & BARS

Bar Carib €€ A restaurant serving three meals daily, with a swimming pool and tennis court (racket and balls for hire). The special barbecue (Sun lunchtime and Wed evening) is a bargain, but book ahead. Sandwiches and children's meals also available.
ⓐ Montinhos da Luz, 1 km (0.6 miles) from Praia da Luz ❶ 282 78 89 08
🕒 Open 10.00–late, closed in winter

Bar Habana The International Café Whatever it is, they have it at this all-day–all-night meeting spot on the beach. Breakfast at all hours, with burgers, curry, Chinese favourites, ice cream and an extensive cocktail list. 🕒 Open 09.00–02.00

Cangalho €€–€€€ Portuguese cuisine served in a traditional farmhouse setting. Home-baked bread, roast suckling pig and chicken *cabidela* (stewed in a rich sauce with rice) are among the specialities here. ⓐ Quinta Figueiras, Sítio do Medronho, Barão de São João ❶ 282 69 72 18 🕒 Open noon–15.00 and 18.00–22.00, closed Mon

Dolphin €€–€€€ Restaurant with sea views from the patio, serving Portuguese/international cuisine, plus some interesting South African specials. Desserts are outstanding. ⓐ Rua da Calheta 14A ❶ 282 78 99 92 🕒 Open 18.30–22.00 (last meal order), closed Dec–Jan

Duke of Holland €–€€ English-run bar and restaurant offering all kinds of food, from snacks to full meals. Steaks in sauces are their speciality. Quiz and karaoke nights. ⓐ Rua da Praia 19 ❶ 282 78 98 88 🕒 Open 19.00–02.00

Esplanada da Fortaleza €€ This terrace restaurant serves modern international cooking, including inventive pizzas, lots of vegetarian choices and great cakes during the day. Wonderful views to the rocky beach below. 🕒 Open 10.00–22.00

Fortaleza da Luz €€€ Housed in a beautifully restored, very atmospheric 16th-century fortress, this Portuguese restaurant, with fantastic views of the coast, is perfect for that special romantic occasion. Live jazz during Sun lunch in summer. ⓐ Rua da Igreja 3 ⓣ 282 78 99 26 ⓛ Open 12.30–15.00 and 19.00–22.00 (last meal order)

Godots €€–€€€ English-run restaurant offering grilled meat and fish as well as vegetarian dishes on a predominantly international menu. The atmosphere is relaxed, and you can choose to dine alfresco on the terrace. ⓐ Rua 25 de Abril ⓣ 282 78 96 47 ⓔ godotsagain@hotmail.com ⓛ Open 19.00–22.00 (last meal order), closed Sun and Wed

Maharaja da Luz €€ Restaurant serving up good northern-Indian food with a takeaway service. ⓐ Centro Commercial, Edificio Luz Tur (above the pharmacy) ⓣ 282 78 95 79 ⓛ Open noon–14.30 and 18.00–midnight

Vai a Remos €–€€ Uncomplicated cuisine, featuring roast suckling pig, roast kid and fresh seafood. Perfect for families with young children, as there is an enclosed area in full view of parents where youngsters can play. ⓐ Off EN 125 ⓣ 282 78 23 85 ⓛ Open Tues–Sun 11.30–22.00

NIGHTLIFE
The Bull Crowded pub with a pricey upstairs restaurant featuring fine views of the rocky beach. ⓐ Rua da Calheta 5

Le Privé Club serving up a mix of Portuguese and English pop music, especially popular with teenagers. ⓐ Rua José da Conceição Conde, beneath Centro Commercial Via Sul ⓛ Open 23.00–04.00

Rocha Negra Popular beach bar right on the sands. ⓛ Open until 02.00

Alvor
picture-postcard resort

Perfect for a relaxing holiday, Alvor is a very pretty resort, handy for the nightclubs of Praia da Rocha on the one hand, and for the historic sights of Lagos on the other.

The focal point of Alvor is **Torralta Beach**, a 1 km (0.6 mile) stretch of fine golden sand with sun loungers, umbrellas and pedalos to rent. A 15-minute stroll over the hill brings you to the old village. Here the fishermen bring their catches to market at dawn, while villagers collect shellfish from the estuary. On the other side of the harbour is the 16th-century parish church with typical Manueline stone carvings.

THINGS TO SEE & DO
Ethnographical Museum ★
Tiny, old-fashioned museum next to the small church of Santa Casa de Misericórdia, tracing Alvor's fishing roots. ❸ Rua Marquês de Pombal ● Open daily ❶ Small admission fee

Folk dancing ★
The **Hotel Delfim** alternates evenings of folk dancing and traditional *fado* music on Tuesdays. ❸ Praia dos Três Irmãos ❶ 282 45 89 01

Golf ★★
Laid out on sandstone cliffs with superb views, **Alto Golf** is a taxing 73-par course, designed by Sir Henry Cotton and famous for its 604 m (660 yd) 16th hole, one of the longest in Europe. There is also a golf school with practice bunker. ❸ Quinto do Alto do Paco ❶ 282 41 69 13

Helicopter Flights ★
SkyZone offers sightseeing and photography flights over the beaches and cliffs. Or you can sit back in the **Sky Café** and watch the small planes land and take off at Penina Airport, 1 km (0.6 miles) from Alvor. ❶ 282 49 59 26

🔺 *Alvor's parish church looks like it is made of icing-sugar*

Horse riding & jeep safaris ★★
Vale de Ferro Riding offers scenic, cross-country excursions through the hinterland of Portimão. Beginners and experienced riders are all welcome. Jeep safaris can also be arranged into the mountains at Monchique. Ⓦ www.horseridingalgarveportugal.com

Lawn bowling & tennis ★
The **San António Lawn Bowling and Country Club** has tennis and squash courts, swimming pools, a sauna, a Turkish bath, aerobic classes and a beauty salon. There are special-offer prices to include two to three hours' bowling and lunch. ⓐ Montes de Alvor ⓣ 282 49 57 13 Ⓛ Restaurant and bar open 10.00–22.00 (09.30–19.00 in winter)

Ten-pin bowling ★
Torralta Bowling has four bowling lanes, snooker, pool, pinball machines and a bar. ⓐ Praia de Alvor ⓣ 282 45 86 63 Ⓛ Open 14.00–02.00

Wetlands ★★
The estuaries of the Alvor and the Odiáxere are rich in birdlife, and (for the time being at least) protected from developers. Explore the salt pans via the raised footpath.

RESTAURANTS & BARS

Albar €–€€ Despite its snack-bar appearance, the Albar serves very good Portuguese and international full meals. The atmosphere is lively but not hectic, service is friendly and fast, and it's a perfect place for people-watching. ⓐ Rua Marquês de Pombal 21 ☎ 282 45 71 24 🕒 Open 10.00–late

Alvila €€–€€€ A long-established restaurant, renowned for its Portuguese/international food, flambéed desserts and *fado* every Tues. ⓐ Amoreira-Alvor (near Hotel Delfim) ☎ 282 45 87 75 🕒 Open 12.30–14.30 and 19.00–22.30, closed Wed ❶ Free transport on *fado* nights

L'Angolo Ristorante Italiano €–€€ A charming, small pizza-pasta house by the church. Friendly staff, nice atmosphere. ⓐ Rua 28 de Septembro ☎ 282 45 83 69 🕒 Open 11.00–15.00 and 18.30–late, closed Tues

Calypso Fun Bar € Burgers and sandwiches are served, along with drinks a-plenty at this bar. ⓐ In front of the Carlton Hotel's driving range 🕒 Open 09.30–02.00

Casa da Mare €€ Clams or fish in a *cataplana* and seafood kebabs are the specialties of this popular seafood house. ⓐ Largo da Ribeira 10 ☎ 282 45 81 91

China Garden €€ The food here is excellent quality, beautifully presented and very good value. Friendly staff and a nice relaxed dining room. ⓐ Rua Dr Alfonso Costa 43 ☎ 282 45 72 84 🕒 Open noon–15.00 and 18.00–23.30

Fonte de Pedra €–€€ International dishes and Portuguese cuisine are served at this restaurant in the countryside with rustic decor. ⓐ Alcalar ☎ 282 47 10 34 🕒 Open 11.00–21.00, closed Wed– Thurs

Hang Zhou Chinese Restaurant €€–€€€ Choose the airy terrace or the elegant interior and feast on aromatic crispy duck.
🅐 Just uphill from the main roundabout ☏ 282 45 98 88

Hellman's €€ Imaginative Portuguese/international cuisine in a cosy traditional house. The top floor has great views. 🅐 Travessa da Ribeira ☏ 282 45 82 08 🕒 Open 11.30–15.00 and 18.00–22.30

Os Marafados €€ In an old house, this restaurant-bar serves large plates of international food and is always packed.
🅐 Rua Dr Frederico Ramos Mendes ☏ 282 45 72 65 🕒 Open 10.00–late

Somewhere Else €–€€€ Cook your own fish or meat on a stone grill in this cosmopolitan, upstairs Irish-Dutch-run restaurant.
🅐 Rua Poeta João de Deus ☏ 282 45 85 95 🕒 Open noon–23.00

Tasca Morais €–€€ The friendly staff at this charming, old-fashioned house serve good local food. 🅐 Rua Dr António José de Almeida 14 ☏ 282 45 93 92 🕒 Open 18.30–22.30, closed Wed

 Vagabundo €€–€€€ The nicest dining room in town, set in a traditional house with a large open aspect and lovely garden. Excellent Portuguese/international menu (try the Madeira kebab).
🅐 Rua Dr Frederico Ramos Mendes ☏ 282 45 87 26 🕒 Open 18.00–22.30

NIGHTLIFE

Borala There is live music nightly from 22.00 in this trendy bar.
🅐 Rua Dr Fredrico Ramos Mendes 17

Mourisco Bar Moorish-themed bar with cheap beer and good service. Lively by night. 🅐 Rua Dr Frederico Ramos Mendes

Paddy's Bar Irish-style bar with a rooftop terrace and guitarist.
🅐 Rua Dr António José de Almeida 9

○ *The 'beach of the rocks'*

Praia da Rocha
fun resort

Praia da Rocha (pronounced 'Pryah da Rosha') is shamelessly brash, a fun resort with generous helpings of sun, sea and sand. The name means 'beach of the rocks', an allusion to the spectacular outcrops of red and yellow sandstone that feature on so many postcards. There's more than enough room for sunbathers on the 100 m (110 yd) wide swathe of sand, but just to make sure, a tunnel carved through the west cliff opens up the more secluded bays beyond.

THINGS TO SEE & DO
Fortaleza da Santa Caterina ★★

This 1691 fortress offers spectacular views at sunset – beach and ocean on one side, marina on the other. There is also a small garden below, with beach views. ⓐ Avenida Tomás Cabreira ⓒ Open daily ⓘ Free admission

Rocha Express ★★
The tourist train leaves the Miradouro every 30 minutes, calling at
Fortaleza and Praia do Vau. Tickets can be bought on board.
🕐 Open 10.00–noon and 16.00–23.30

Ten-pin bowling ★
Praia da Rocha bowling alley has four lanes, plus video games, pool, table
football and a bar. 🅐 Avenida Tomás Cabreira 🕐 Open 10.00–02.00

Water sports ★★
Water skiing and pedalo rental (including snorkels) are all available from
the beach. Praia da Rocha also has excellent conditions for windsurfing –
boards can be rented by the hour, with lessons for beginners.

SHOPPING
There are two supermarkets, **Alisuper** and **Himalaia**, on
Avenida Tomás Cabreira. There is a **gypsy market** on the
road to Portimão (close to Clube Praia da Rocha) on the first
Monday of each month.

RESTAURANTS

Cabassa €€ Set on a lawn at the quiet eastern part of the
seafront, this is a delightful terrace restaurant known for its
high-quality inventive Italian cooking and excellent barbecue nights.
Speedy, friendly service. 🅐 Avenida Tomás Cabreira 🕐 282 42 43 07
🕐 Open 18.00–late

Cantinho Tropical €–€€ Brazilian specialities and local seafood
predominate on the menu of this attractive restaurant. One of
their specialities, *moqueca de camarão*, is a Brazilian shrimp dish. 🅐 Alto
da Quinta 🕐 282 41 32 43 🕐 Open Mon, Wed, Thurs 19.00–midnight,
Fri–Sun noon–17.00 and 19.00–midnight, closed Tues

A Casa de Rocha €€–€€€ Highly rated restaurant set in a 1930s summer villa, serving top-quality shellfish and Portuguese specials. ⓐ Sitio dos Castelos, Avenida Tomás Cabreira ① 282 41 96 74 ① Open Tues–Sun noon–15.00 and 18.00–22.00 (closed Sun lunch)

Casalinho €€ It may not look much, but this place has a loyal army of fans who come here for top-quality Portuguese/international cooking with flambé specials. ⓐ Main beach, down steps by the Penguin (see below) ① 282 42 25 79 ① Open 09.30–22.30

Churrasqueira € Cheap and cheerful café with great views of the beach and coast. Chicken *piri-piri* (a spicy African-influenced dish, see page 94) is the speciality. ⓐ Avenida Tomás Cabreira ① 282 49 19 93

Fagin's € Takeaway fish and chip shop with fish fingers for children and mouthwatering spit-roasted chicken. ⓐ Edificio Rochamar ① Open 09.00–midnight

Nova China €–€€ Reasonably priced Chinese with an excellent takeaway service. ⓐ Edificio San José, Avenida Tomás Cabreira ① 282 41 54 04 ① Open noon–15.00 and 18.00–late

Oliver's € Authentic English food, from breakfasts to Sunday roast. ⓐ Edificio Rochamar ① 282 41 18 62 ① Open 09.00–02.00

Pizzaria La Dolce Vita € This pasta and pizza restaurant has more than two dozen pizza varieties to choose from. Look for bargain lunch specials and their Italian ice cream. ⓐ Avenida Tomás Cabreira, opposite the Hotel Algarve Casino ① 282 41 94 44

O Terraço de Penguin €€ Long-established, the Penguin is the nicest place to eat in town, with a magnificently sited terrace, great service, and an adventurous menu with good vegetarian choices. ⓐ Avenida Tomás Cabreira ① 282 48 36 23 ① Open noon–midnight

Titanic €€€ Dress up for a special evening out at this relaxing flambé and fish restaurant, with a wide choice of international dishes. ⓐ Rua Eng Francisco Bivar ⓣ 282 42 23 71

The Village Inn €€–€€€ Seating 30 in a friendly atmosphere, this restaurant serves delicious food, with a strong emphasis on vegetarian dishes. ⓐ Mexilhoeira da Carregação, about 2 km (1.2 miles) east of Portimão, on the other bank of the River Arade ⓣ 282 41 20 36 ⓛ Open Tues–Sat 18.30–22.00, closed Sun and Mon ⓘ Reservations recommended

NIGHTLIFE

Babylone Lively disco club with a large dance floor. ⓐ Edificio Tropical Rocha ⓛ Open 23.00–06.00

Casino American roulette, French roulette, Black Jack, Punto e Banca and 306 slot machines will relieve you of your euros here. Dinner is served at 20.30 nightly, followed by a Las Vegas-style show at 22.30. ⓐ Hotel Algarve, Avenida Tomás Cabreira ⓣ 282 35 73 81 ⓛ Open 16.00–04.00 ⓘ Passport required

Colombus Disco bar known for its cocktails. ⓐ Edificio Rio a Vista ⓛ Open until 04.00

Katedral Large nightclub with bars, Satellite TV, pool tables and disco featuring several different music styles. ⓐ Avenida Tomás Cabreira ⓛ Open 23.00–07.30

On the Rocks Praia da Rocha's trendiest cocktail bar and disco, with terrace overlooking the beach. ⓐ Avenida Tomás Cabreira ⓛ Open 10.00–04.00, happy hour 10.00–20.30

Taffy's Bar Sports bar with large screen. ⓐ Avenida Tomás Cabreira ⓛ Open until 02.00

RESORTS

Armação de Pêra
the Algarve's longest beach

Palm trees shade the promenade at Armação de Pêra (pronounced 'Armasau de Perra'), a modern resort boasting one of the longest expanses of sand in the Algarve. In fact, it stretches all the way to Galé, a satellite of Albufeira.

To the east of the resort is Fisherman's Beach where, early in the morning, small colourful boats depart, as they have done for centuries, in search of the day's catch. Get here at about 10.00 hours to see them return with their booty. The old part of town lies in the cobbled streets behind the beach, and here you'll find the local bars and fish restaurants. To the west of the resort are the Algarve's classic rock stacks and cliffs. Boat trips from the beach pass these on their way to the spectacular stacks and caves between here and Carvoeiro (see page 32).

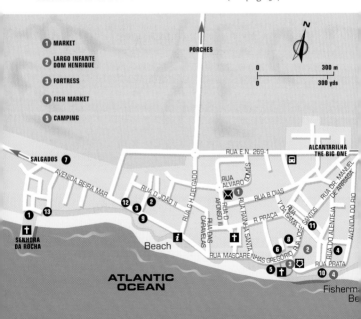

THINGS TO SEE & DO
Alcantarilha ★

Alcantarilha has a notorious traffic bottleneck on the EN 125. Get off the main road here and go to the landmark church, which has a macabre chapel lined with human skulls and bones. There is nothing sinister about this. They are simply the remains of some 1500 parishioners, permanently exhibited as a cheerful reminder of human mortality!

The Big One – Aqualand ★★★

Portugal's largest water park offers aquatic rides and amusements in a garden setting. Not just for kids, there is entertainment for all the family.
ⓐ EN 125, at Alcantarilha ❶ 282 32 02 30 Ⓦ www.bigone-waterpark.com

Golf ★★★

Salgados is a links-style 18-hole course of 6080 m (over 6750 yards). Handicap certificate required. ⓐ Vale de Parra ❶ 289 58 30 30

Senhora da Rocha ★★

'Our Lady of the Rock' is a sailor's chapel, dating from the 16th century, perched on a spectacular headland approximately 3 km (1.8 miles) west of the resort. If you make the effort to climb up to the chapel, the interior contains some lovely *azulejos* (tiles) and votive model-ship offerings (check opening times first with the tourist office in Armação de Pêra). A rock-cut tunnel gives access to the lovely beach of Senhora da Rocha.

SHOPPING

The small town of **Porches**, just inland from Armação de Pêra (a few kilometres before you reach Lagoa), is famous for its pottery (see page 99). Here you will have the opportunity to watch the potters at work before purchasing genuine hand-painted ceramics from any of the outlets situated along the main EN 125 highway.

🔺 *Fresh fish, straight from the sea, to boat, to restaurant*

RESTAURANTS & BARS (see map on page 28)

Casa d'Italia €€ ❶ Imagine yourself as the guest in a private country villa as you enjoy authentic Italian food at shaded tables set around a pool, with hillside and sea views. Quality at surprisingly modest prices. ➌ Ald Porches Praia, Sra da Rocha (signposted opposite Hotel Viking) ➊ 282 31 08 47 ➏ Open 10.30–midnight, meals served 12.30–15.00 and 19.00–22.30

O Fernando €€ ❷ Excellent fish dishes are served in this typical Portuguese restaurant. Try the grilled fresh salmon. ➌ Rua Rosa dos Ventos ➊ 282 31 34 81 ➏ Open 10.00–midnight

Gelataria Penguin € ❸ A promenade café selling ice creams, crêpes, sandwiches and other snacks. ➌ Avenida Beira Mar

A Grelha €€ ❹ It claims to be the oldest traditional restaurant in the Algarve – it's certainly one of the best for fresh fish and seafood, though it also offers a good selection of meat dishes. ➌ Rua do Alentejo 2 ➊ 282 31 22 45 ➏ Open noon–15.00 and 18.00–22.00/22.30

Jony Beach Bar €€ ❺ A great setting for inexpensive fresh fish and seafood, or just a drink and a snack. ➌ Beachfront, by Fortaleza (fortress) ➊ 282 34 22 01 ➏ Open 10.00–23.00

Kam Kong €€ **6** Excellent Chinese food. Specialities include crispy duck with pancakes. ⓐ Largo 25 de Abril ⓣ 282 31 21 96 ⓛ Open 18.00–midnight

Ocean €€€ **7** This is your chance to wear that little black dress or jacket and tie you brought. Located in the 5-star Hotel Villa Vita complex, dinners are by reservation only. You won't be disappointed; the cuisine is as stunning as the ocean views. ⓐ Vila Vita Parc, Alporchinhos ⓣ 289 31 01 00 ⓛ Open 17.30–22.00

Pizzaria Gabi € **8** Cheap and cheerful pizzeria for when you want a simple but satisfying snack. ⓐ Rua José António Santos ⓣ 282 31 28 83 ⓛ Open noon–late

Raj €–€€ **9** Excellent value Indian cuisine in a wonderful setting – with great views from the patio overlooking the sea. ⓐ Hotel Garbe ⓣ 282 32 02 60 ⓛ Open 12.30–14.30 and 18.30–23.30

O Serol €€ **10** At the entrance to the fisherman's quarter, Serol is highly recommended for its fish, shellfish and various *cataplanas* (indoor dining only). ⓐ Rua Portas do Mar 2 ⓣ 282 31 21 46 ⓛ Open noon–15.30 and 19.00–22.30, closed Wed

NIGHTLIFE

Havanna **11** Trendy cocktail bar with resident parrot. ⓐ Rua Dr Martinho Simoes ⓛ Open 19.00–late

The Runner **12** Friendly, English-style pub with satellite TV, bar meals and snacks served all day. ⓐ Avenida Beira Mar ⓛ Open 11.00–late

Sebastian's **13** Located in the Hotel Viking, the only nightclub in Armação de Pêra takes an underworld theme for its decor. ⓐ Hotel Viking, Senhora da Rocha ⓛ Open Fri–Sat 21.30–late

Carvoeiro
sandy coves and sea caves

Armação de Pêra's smaller neighbour, Carvoeiro (pronounced 'Carvowheroh') is highly photogenic, with brightly painted fishing boats and spruced-up, whitewashed villas. Reached by a long and narrow valley road, which eventually ends in a pocket-handkerchief of golden sand, Carvoeiro is one of the prettiest resorts in the Algarve.

THINGS TO SEE & DO
Horse riding ★
Casa Galaraz stable has a special park for children. Experienced staff offer guided horse rides and instruction. ❸ Estrada de Benagil, near the beach at Carvoeiro ❶ 282 35 80 55

Slide and Splash ★★★
Whirlpools and waterslides, including the new 'Black Hole', are among the features of this popular fun park. Facilities include shops, bars and a restaurant. Slide and Splash runs a bus service with pick-up points all along the coast (ask the tourist office for further details).
❸ N 125, Vale de Deus, Estombar ❶ 282 34 16 85 ❷ Open 10.00–18.00
❶ Admission charge

SHOPPING

 A Praça Velha, the 'old market', deals mostly in mass-produced pottery, though there are other handicrafts and souvenirs for sale. ❸ Rua dos Pescadores ◷ Open daily
For better quality pottery go to **Porches** (see pages 29 and 99). The nearest real market is at **Lagoa** (second Sunday of each month). Also on the main EN 125 at Lagoa is **Mundo do Sapato** (Shoe World), with some bargain brand-name footwear.

Tennis ★★
Performance Tennis School has lessons for all levels, whether learning to play or improving your game; set in a beautiful location. ❶ 282 35 78 47

Wine tasting ★
Lagoa is famous for rough red wines with a high alcohol content.
The Lagoa Wine Co-operative, on the Portimão road, opens its cellars for conducted tours and wine tastings. ❶ 282 34 21 81 ◷ Usually open 09.30–12.30 and 14.00–17.30, but call to check ❶ It is advisable to book at least 24 hours in advance

BEACHES
Rocky promontories and crumbling sandstone cliffs, concealing a succession of inviting coves and grottoes, characterize this stretch of coastline. The gently shelving beach at **Vale de Centianes** (approached by a flight of steps) is excellent for surfing. At **Algar Seco**, the cliff forms a double arch, bridging the entrance to a cavernous lagoon of deep, clear water – a snorkeller's paradise. A small road train, the *Jumbolino*, travels the 4 km (2.5 miles) east to **Praia do Carvalho** (also known as Smugglers Cove), but two other beaches well worth going that extra mile or so for are the coves of **Praia de Benagil** and **Praia da Marinha**.

◀ *Carvoeiro's sheltered cove*

GOLFING

Vale de Milho Designed by Ryder Cup player Dave Thomas, architect of the Belfry Brabazon Course in Warwickshire, England, this is an attractive course and surprisingly challenging for every golfer. Water hazards play a part in four of the nine holes on the par-30 course. Ideal for practising your short game and excellent value for money. ☏ 282 35 85 02

Pinta Pestana Golf Resort A new, well-designed 18-hole course, built around an ancient olive grove with a great mountain backdrop. Although it is a championship-class course, it is suitable for all handicap levels.

The renowned **David Leadbetter Golf Academy** is also based here, along with its practice areas, shop, restaurant and bar. ☏ 282 34 09 00

RESTAURANTS

Happy's €€ This cheerful Dutch-run restaurant serves a selection of international and Portuguese specialities in a friendly, cosy atmosphere. ⓐ Estrada do Farol ☏ 282 35 76 92 🕒 Open Mon–Sat noon–23.00, closed Sun

Maxime €€ Fresh seasonal produce and seafood are prepared with French and Dutch influences. Be sure to check the daily specials board. ⓐ Estrada do Farol 15 ☏ 282 35 78 52 🕒 Open 18.00–late, closed Wed

Oasis € The varied menu is perfect for families who can't agree on dinner. All dishes are budget-friendly. ⓐ Near the beach at Rua do Barranco 34 ☏ 282 35 73 32 ⓦ www.restaurantoasis.com

Palacio do Cône € Serves ice cream and reasonably priced pancakes with a variety of toppings. ⓐ Praia da Carvoeiro

Piu Churrasqueira €€ Steaks, ribs, kebabs, sardines and vegetable dishes are all grilled at this sea-view restaurant. ⓐ Largo do Carvoeiro ⓣ 282 35 05 90 ⓦ www.praiacarvoeiro.com

Piu Grand Café € This café serves breakfast and lunch, with sandwiches and simple main dishes. ⓐ Largo do Carvoeiro ⓣ 282 35 05 90 ⓦ www.praiacarvoeiro.com

Primavera €–€€ Mediterranean dishes, more than half of which are Italian inspired, fill the menu of this bright, attractive restaurant. In the summer steaks and pasta are served in a shaded beer garden. ⓐ Rua das Flores 2 ⓣ 282 35 83 42 ⓛ Open 18.30–late, closed Wed

Stone Steak €€–€€€ Cook your steak, fish or prawns the healthy and tasty way on sizzling stone grills. ⓐ Monte Carvoeiro ⓣ 282 35 77 30 ⓛ Open 18.00–23.00

NIGHTLIFE

Jailhouse Set in a converted wine cellar, this is Portugal's first disco, featuring nightly live music and dance-floor favourites going back to the 1960s. It also has a beer garden. ⓐ Rua do Escondidinho 9 ⓛ Open 18.00–late

Manoel's Jazz Club Manoel and his sax have attained folk-hero status, creating this excellent jazz club. ⓐ Monte Carvoeiro ⓛ Open 22.30–late

Round-up Saloon A great place for country-and-western fans and line dancing (Mon). Enjoy snacks, inexpensive drinks, karaoke and live piano music. ⓐ Estrada do Farol ⓣ 282 35 70 09 ⓛ Open 18.00–02.00

Sully's An Irish pub, serving full English breakfast in the morning, and pub food all day. ⓐ Rua do Paraiso 2 ⓣ 282 35 77 87 ⓦ www.carvoeiro.com/sullys ⓛ Open 09.00–02.00

6 MARKET

SAMORA BARROS

C. AGUAS

AVENIDA DO TÉNIS

DR. DIOGO LEOTE

RUA 1 DE DEZEMBRO

GALE
CASTELLO
SESMARIAS
9

T. C. AGUAS
11

Praia de
Albufeira

4
RUA LATINO COELHO
✝

RUA PADRE SEMEDO

FERREIRAS
ALGOZ

✝

1

AV. 5 DE 1 OUTUBRO

AV. DA LIBERDADE

TUNNEL
TO BEACH

ℹ ✉

PRAÇA
REPÚBLICA

LARGO ENGHENHEIRO
DUARTE PACHECO

TOWN HALL

✝

RUA JOAQUIM PEDRO

7 GALERIA DE
ARTE PINTO
SAMORA BARROS

RUA JOSÉ BERNARDINO DA BATERIA

OLD
VILLAGE

RUA CANDIDO DOS REIS

AV. 23 DE ABRIL

RUA ALVES CORREIA

2

8

3
10
13
12

RUA C. HERCULANO

RUA DOS TELHEIROS

Praia dos
Pescadores

LARGO CAIS
HERCULANO

FISH AUCTION

➤ Z
0   50 100 m
0   100 yds

PIER

5
↓
PRAIA DA OURA
MONTECHORO

RUA SACADURA CABRAL

MONTECHO
OURA BE

Albufeira
old Moorish town

One of the liveliest resorts in the Algarve, Albufeira (pronounced 'Ahl-boo-fair-a') was called 'castle on the sea' by the Moors. The charm of the original fishing village has been preserved in the twists and turns of cobbled lanes, lined with pretty, whitewashed houses.

BEACHES

At the **Praia dos Pescadores** (Fishermen's Beach), local fishermen unload their catch, mend their nets and occasionally touch up the paintwork on their boats. There are fish auctions here, daily, from 08.00 to 10.00 hours. The main town beach, approached by a tunnel cut through the rock, is excellent for swimming and sunbathing but tends to become crowded. To the west are the smaller beaches of **São Rafael**, **Coelha** and **Castelo**.

THINGS TO SEE & DO
Diving ★★

PADI-certified **Atlantic Diving** offers lessons for beginners as well as more challenging trips for experienced divers. ☎ 289 58 74 79 ⓦ www.atlantic-diving.com. Another choice is the **Tivoli Dive Center** ☎ 965 21 91 83 ⓦ www.tivoli-diving.com)

Galeria de Arte Pinto Samora Barros ★

This gallery features works by Samora Barros, a resident artist specializing in relief paintings of Portuguese themes. ➌ Largo Engenheiro Duarte Pacheco ⓛ Open 16.30–23.00 (July–mid-Sept) and 10.30–17.00 (mid-Sept–June), closed Sun in low season ⓘ Free admission

Krazy Golf ★★

The course is set in subtropical gardens and lakes, where pedalo rides are part of the fun. Other attractions include a Quad circuit, an exotic animal farm and swimming pools. ➌ Algoz, 30 min from Albufeira by car or bus ⓛ Open 09.30–23.00 (June–Sept); 09.30–19.00 (Oct–May)

RESTAURANTS (see map on page 36)
The heart of the town's nightlife is the pedestrianized square of Largo Enghenheiro Duarte Pacheco, lined with restaurants and bars. On summer nights there is a carnival atmosphere here, with stalls lit by fairy lights selling arts, crafts and souvenirs, and crowds of visitors thronging the narrow alleyways.

Adega Dom Pipas €€ **1** Long-established popular Portuguese restaurant tucked in a tiny alleyway just off the main drag. Together next-door **A Travessa**, its outdoor tables create something of a street-party atmosphere. ⓐ Travessa dos Arcos ☎ 289 58 80 91 🕒 Open noon–15.00 and 18.00–22.00

Anna's €€–€€€ **2** Set in a charming old fisherman's cottage in the heart of the old town, just above the beach, Anna's has been going strong since the 1970s, serving up high-quality, adventurous, international cooking. The food is always delicious. ⓐ Rua Nova 7 ☎ 289 51 35 58/917 8 8 82 11 (for reservations) 🕒 Open 18.00–late, closed Thurs

Cabana Fresca €€ **3** Carefully prepared food is served on a terrace overlooking the water. ⓐ Praia dos Pescadores ☎ 289 58 54 56

O Dias € **4** Good-value Portuguese grills on a small terrace with wonderful views. Book a seat as close to the cliff top as possible. ⓐ Praça Miguel Bombarda ☎ 289 51 52 46 🕒 Open noon–15.00 and 18.00–22.00, closed Thurs

O Licorne €€–€€€ **5** The food at this restaurant is excellent, with an atmosphere to match. Tables are well spaced in front of a hearty fireplace. Vegetarian dishes are always available. ⓐ Estrada de Albufeira, between Albufeira and Olhos d'Agua ☎ 917 31 32 07 🕒 Open Mon–Sat from 18.30

O Marinheiro €€ **6** A class act, run by a Swiss/Portuguese couple. The wine cellar is outstanding. ❸ West of the old town, near Galé ❶ 289 59 23 50 ❶ Bookings are essential

Pampas Steakhouse €€–€€€ **7** This Argentinian-style restaurant occupies an attractive terrace on the corner of the main square and serves the best steaks in town. ❸ Largo Enghenheiro Duarte Pacheco 53 ❶ 289 51 23 20 ❷ Open 09.00–02.00

A Ruina €€€ **8** This is perhaps Albufeira's most famous restaurant, a labyrinth of ancient rooms serving top-quality fish and shellfish. There is also a terrace overlooking Fishermen's Beach. ❸ Rua Cais Herculano ❶ 289 51 20 94 ❷ Open 12.30–15.00 and 19.00–23.00

Vila Joya €€€ **9** Dress up and bring your credit cards to this Michelin two-star restaurant. It's pricey, but the excellent cuisine, beautifully prepared and presented, is worth it. And the view from the terrace is not bad either. ❸ Praia da Gale ❶ 289 59 17 95

NIGHTLIFE

7½ **10** If you fancy a change from Kiss Disco (see page 58), this is the place to be seen in the wee small hours in Albufeira old town. ❸ Rua Cais Herculano ❷ Open 21.00–late

Bizarro **11** Slightly Bohemian and nicely laid-back, with live acoustic Brazilian guitar music every Tues. Fantastic cliff-top views. ❸ Esplanada 30 ❶ 289 51 28 24 ❷ Open 10.00–late, closed Sun

Jo Jo's **12** Lively, friendly English-owned boozer with multiple TV screens. Fish and chips and Sunday roasts. ❸ Rua Gonçales de Lagos 1 ❿ www.jojosbar.com ❷ Open 10.00–16.00 and 18.30–late

Snoopy's Bar **13** Bands play here most nights until the early hours of the morning. The terrace overlooks Fisherman's Beach. ❶ 289 51 53 75

🔺 *The marina – Vilamoura's focal point*

Vilamoura
marina and golf

This modern, purpose-built resort is one of the most popular in the Algarve. Low-rise apartment-hotels painted in pastel shades, broad, tree-lined avenues and tastefully landscaped parks and gardens lead to the marina, the town's focal point, where every conceivable amenity can be found.

The marina at Vilamoura is the largest in Portugal, with berths for up to 1500 yachts. Boats leave from the quayside to explore the fascinating Algarvian coastline, with its myriad coves, beaches and unusual rock formations – some yachts will take you as far as Portimão and back. Big-game fishing (blue shark, tuna and record-breaking black marlin) is also popular, while the water sports on offer include scuba diving, water skiing and windsurfing. The marina is a place for people-watching, window shopping or promenading, especially at night when the entire harbour is illuminated. Souvenir outlets and chic boutiques alternate with smartly turned out cafés and terrace restaurants, offering everything from pizzas and pancakes to chow mein and chicken *piri-piri*. Karaoke is a popular form of entertainment in the family-friendly bars, which stay open well into the small hours.

The **Condor de Vilamoura**, a handsome replica of a 19th-century fishing schooner, takes passengers on half- or full-day excursions along the coast and on romantic evening cruises. Children under six travel free and the price includes a barbecue lunch on a remote beach.

THINGS TO SEE & DO
Balloons and Boats ★
Get a new perspective of Vilamoura and the surrounding coast from the air or water. **Vistarama Flyer** (❶ 289 31 65 76) offers short ascents by balloon at reasonable prices, and the well-equipped **Cacador Azul** (❶ 289 31 52 34) takes hopeful fishing parties in search of marlin, shark, tuna and bottom fish.

Cerro da Vila ★
Vilamoura means 'Moorish village', but the town's origins date back to Roman times. A new museum has been built around the remains, which include a villa, a farm and baths, and displays the coins, mosaics and other artefacts found here. ❸ Avenida Cerro da Vila ❶ 289 31 21 53 ❹ Open 10.00–13.00 and 17.00–23.30 ❶ Admission charge

Golf ★★★
Vilamoura's five courses will appeal to experienced golfers and novices alike. The refurbished **Old Course** has testing narrow fairways laid out between umbrella pines. **Pinhal** has beautiful sea views, while the bunkers and water hazards of **Laguna** present plenty of challenges. **The Millennium course** opened in 2000, and the fifth debuted in 2004 – Arnold Palmer's **Victoria**.

Roma Golf Park If you're not quite up to the Old Course at Vilamoura, try this excellent little crazy golf course themed to the Roman finds next door at the Cerro da Vila museum. Two lots of 18 holes are surrounded by fountains and pools. Tournaments for seniors and juniors on Sundays. 🕐 Open 10.00–midnight

Health & fitness ★

The Rock Garden is a state-of-the-art sports centre with indoor and outdoor swimming pools, squash and tennis courts, a Turkish bath, full-size snooker tables, table tennis, darts, a gym and a fitness suite. ⓐ Aldeia do Campo, Vilamoura ☎ 289 32 27 40

Horse riding ★★

For lessons with qualified, English-speaking instructors and equipment rental, contact **Horses Paradise** in Almancil, which claims to be the longest-established riding centre in the Algarve, and specializes in leading small groups through beautiful countryside. ☎ 289 39 41 89

Tennis ★★

Vilamoura Ténis Centre is a high-quality facility offering lessons, tournaments and 12 courts for hire (five floodlit). ☎ 289 30 23 69

RESTAURANTS & BARS

🍴 **19th Hole** €–€€ Friendly Portuguese-managed English-style pub with satellite TV and a nice position right in the corner of the marina. It dispenses English beers, full meals, snacks and kebabs as well as traditional Portuguese dishes. ⓐ Marina de Vilamoura ☎ 289 30 11 13 🕐 Open 09.00–02.00

🔲 **Akvavit** €€€ Typical of the cosmopolitan nature of the marina, this very highly rated restaurant cooks mostly French and Portuguese dishes, but do look out for its Swedish specials. Classy but informal surroundings. ⓐ Marina de Vilamoura ☎ 289 38 07 12 🕐 Open 10.30–23.30 (lunch, noon–16.00; dinner, 19.00–22.30/23.30)

Bella Italia €€ Ice cream and frozen yogurts are worth the queue. Excellent pizzas, including veggie. ⓐ Marina de Vilamoura

 Chez Carlos €€ A friendly sports-oriented bar and restaurant. ⓐ Parque des Amendoeiras ❶ 289 32 16 44

 CJ's €€–€€€ Restaurant in the tranquil Old Village specializing in fish dishes, steaks and roast suckling pig. Tourist menu available. ❶ 289 38 83 58 ⏰ Open 10.00–late

 Marina del Rei €€ Portuguese and international dishes are featured in this unpretentious eatery behind the Nova Rede Bank. ⓐ Avenida Da Marina 5 ❶ 289 31 60 41 ⏰ Open from 18.00

Ostra D'ouro €–€€ The waiters are among the attractions at this light-hearted grill, as they entertain customers. An extensive menu and a good place to sample the local speciality of grilled sardines. ⓐ Centro Commercial, Marina Plaza ❶ 289 30 10 57 ⓦ www.ostradouro.com

NIGHTLIFE

Blackjack An elegant disco and nightclub, with Ladies Night on Thurs. ⓐ Marina de Vilamoura ❶ 289 38 91 47

Casablanca Enjoy live bands, disco and karaoke in a relaxed atmosphere. ⓐ Parque das Amendoeiras ❶ 289 32 26 80 ⏰ Open daily 18.00–late

Casino de Vilamoura American roulette, French roulette, Portuguese dice, Black Jack and 320 slot machines to try your luck on are just some of the dangers to your wealth in this classy gambling establishment. Dinner is served at 20.30 nightly, followed by a Las Vegas-style show at 22.30. ❶ 289 30 29 99 ⏰ Casino open 16.00–03.00 ❶ Passport required

Quarteira
seaside and gypsy market

Once a typical Algarvian fishing village, Quarteira (pronounced 'Kwer-tay-rah') has become a fully fledged seaside resort that complements its more hip neighbour, Vilamoura, but it is not for those seeking a lively nightlife. There are miles of golden sand stretching, almost without interruption, to Vilamoura in one direction and Vale do Lobo in the other. The shops are concentrated around Avenida Dr Francisco Sá Carneiro, as are the many restaurants and bars specializing in such succulent seafood dishes as *cataplana*. Fishing is still a way of life here: the auctioneers sell off the day's catches in the fish market to the west of the beach. Water sports, golfing, tennis and other leisure amenities are all within easy reach of the resort.

THINGS TO SEE & DO
Atlantic Park ★★

Atlantic Park has all the thrills and spills usually associated with waterslides and tunnels, plus showers, loungers, a snack bar and a children's pool. In the summer there's the added attraction of special family holidays. ❸ Atlantic Park is on road EN 125 (special buses run from here to Quarteira) ❶ 289 39 72 82 ❷ Open 09.30–18.30, closed winter ❶ Admission charge

SHOPPING
 Quarteira's **market** (held every Wednesday) on the east side of the town is one of the largest and most colourful in the region. Fruit and vegetables are the mainstay, but you'll also find clothes, towels, tablecloths and souvenirs, often at bargain prices – try bartering here. For more conventional shopping, head for the pedestrianized precinct leading into Rua Vasco da Gama.

Horse riding ★★

Quinta dos Amigos, a farm just outside Quarteira, has a riding centre with qualified, English-speaking instructors. Riding lessons are available as well as organized rides into the countryside and along the beach. Facilities also include two swimming pools, one for children. ❶ 289 39 33 99

BEACHES

Quarteira's long, sandy beach stretches virtually uninterrupted all the way to Faro. It has excellent bathing conditions. Artificial sea defences keep the water calm for swimming, and the beach is well provided with sun loungers, umbrellas, windbreak screens and pedalos. A leisurely stroll along the promenade is the best introduction to the beach area, with its varied selection of waterfront bars and restaurants.

🔺 *Quarteira's glorious beaches make for relaxing days*

RESTAURANTS

Alphonso's €€€ Professional service and a wide selection of excellent food on the menu make this a place for special occasions. The terrace is very pleasant. ⓐ Rua Albertura Mar ❶ 289 31 46 14 🕒 Closed Mon (Nov–May)

La Cabane €€–€€€ Good French food. ⓐ Rua do Levante ❶ 289 31 38 19 🕒 Open 19.00–22.00

Cantinho do Norte €–€€ The daily specials are excellent value at this rustic restaurant specializing in the cuisine of northern Portugal. Hearty casseroles of duck and rice or beans and sausages join the Algarvian *cataplanas* and other seafood dishes to balance the menu. ⓐ EN 125, Quatro Eastadas ❶ 289 39 73 21 🕒 Open 11.30–15.00 and 18.00–23.00

Caravela €–€€ Smart, large, good-value modern restaurant decorated in traditional style, specializing in monkfish, meat *cataplana* and seafood rice. ⓐ Largo do Mercado 17 ❶ 289 31 22 80 🕒 Open Tues–Sun 12.15–15.00 and 19.15–22.00, closed Mon

Le Club €€ Regional and international dishes are served indoors or on the giant terrace. ⓐ Vila Sol, Alto do Semino ❶ 289 30 21 32

Dallas €–€€ Grilled Portuguese dishes and chicken to eat in or take away. *Fado* every Sunday. ⓐ Avenida Dr Francisco Sá Carneiro ❶ 289 31 32 93 🕒 Open noon–15.00 and 19.00–midnight

Fernando's Hideaway €–€€ A grill and steak-house with a long list of daily specials that include typical Portuguese dishes as well as fish and chips. The steaks are huge and it is renowned for Sunday roasts. There are vegetarian specials and a children's menu. The golfer's breakfast begins at 08.00. ⓐ Rua Mestre Luis ❶ 289 31 56 28 🕒 Open 10.00–midnight (Mar–Oct); 10.00–15.00 and 18.00–23.00 (Nov–Feb)

D'Marcello Argentine Steakhouse Grill €€€ Not just your usual steak-house, this restaurant emphasizes presentation as well as the fabulous flavours of the Pampas, using fine china to frame their artistic creations. *Parrilhada* is a selection of several cuts of Argentinian beef and sausages, a dish prepared for two. The veal spare ribs are succulent. ❷ Rua Gill Eanes 5 (near the fish market) ❶ 289 38 98 10 🕑 Open Tues–Sun 19.00–late, closed Mon

O Pescador €€ This small restaurant serves up grilled meat and fish dishes in a modern dining room opposite the fish market. ❷ Largo das Cortes Reais ❶ 289 31 47 55 🕑 Open noon–15.00 and 19.00–22.00, closed Thurs

A Pizza da Villa €–€€ A real taste of Italy on the Algarve, with pizzas and pasta dishes served in a checked-tablecloth ambiance, or to take away. ❷ Off Avenida Marginal ❶ 289 31 57 70 🕑 Open 10.00–23.00

NIGHTLIFE

D'Artagnan's This place is a typical local bar with bingo, karaoke and live music during the week. ❷ Rua Abertura Mar 🕑 Open 09.00– after midnight

Hero's English bar serving a good selection of food, including English breakfasts, curries and Sunday lunch, with quiz nights and Sky Sports by way of entertainment. ❷ Rua Bartolomeu Dias 33 🕑 Open 11.00–22.00, closed Thurs

Paddy Shack A waterfront bar with live music every night. 🕑 Open 11.00–02.00

Sete This is a popular and busy bar with a restaurant. ❸ The Marina 🕑 Open noon–midnight

◆ *Vale do Lobo golf course*

Vale do Lobo & Quinta do Lago
golfer's paradise

Vale do Lobo (pronounced 'Val doh Lobo') and Quinta do Lago (pronounced 'Keenta doh Lahgo', meaning 'lake side') are two of the Algarve's most exclusive and prestigious resorts. Here, among pine forests and salt-water lakes, are the villas of Portugal's rich and famous, as well as four championship golf courses, miles of golden sand, some of the best sports facilities in the Algarve and a good selection of bars, restaurants and nightclubs.

The water sports centre at Quinta do Lago offers pedalos, kayaks, canoes and rowing boats as well as water skiing. Experts are on hand for lessons in windsurfing and sailing. If none of these appeal, you can always join one of the fishing trips on the lakes.

Capela São Lourenço dos Matos (the Church of Saint Lawrence of The Woods), just outside Almancil (inland a little, north-east of Quinta do Lago), is one of the few to survive the 1755 earthquake. It is decorated from floor to ceiling with the magnificent blue-glazed tiling known as *azulejo* (see page 9). The church is kept locked, but a caretaker lives next door and will open it up for you between the hours of 09.00 and 18.00 (please note that it is not possible to view the church over lunch 13.00–14.30).

THINGS TO SEE & DO

Fitness ★
Facilities at **Barringtons** include a golf academy, with floodlit driving range and instruction, squash courts, cricket nets, a fitness centre, sauna and jacuzzi. ⊘ Vale do Lobo ☎ 289 39 88 81

Horse riding ★★
Paraíso dos Cavalos (Horses' Paradise) is one of the best riding centres in the Algarve. Boots and jockey caps are provided, as are lessons for beginners. Full-moon rides in summer. ☎ 289 39 41 89 🕐 Closed Mon

Karting ★
The **Almancil Karting Circuit** was inaugurated by the late great Ayrton Senna and is a replica of the Jacaregaguá Formula 1 circuit in Brazil. Independent circuit suitable for children aged four and over.
⊘ Almancil ☎ 289 39 98 99 🕐 Open from 10.00

Tennis ★
The **David Lloyd Club** is owned by the former British international. The 12-court complex offers coaching and tournament matches.
⊘ Vale do Lobo ☎ 289 36 69 91

Water sports ★
Watersports Levanta organizes a whole range of activities on both the lake and the sea. ⊘ Quinta do Lago ☎ 289 39 49 29

GOLF COURSES

Pinheiros Altos The first half of the par-72 course is set in woodland, while the second presents some water hazards. ☎ 289 35 99 10

Quinta do Lago Designed by Henry Cotton, the two 18-hole, par-72 courses feature lakes and challenging bunkers. ☎ 289 39 07 00

San Lorenzo Exclusively for the use of guests at the Le Meridian, Dona Filipa and Penina Hotels, this par-72 course is currently rated number two in continental Europe. ☎ 289 39 65 34

Vale do Lobo A scenic course with cliff-top views over the Atlantic. Three nine-hole loops. Par 36+36+35. ☎ 289 39 39 39

RESTAURANTS

 Bistro des L'Arts €€€ Top-quality French/Belgian food in a relaxed bistro setting. ⓐ Ruado Calvario 69, Almancil ☎ 289 39 51 14 🕐 Open Mon–Sat noon–15.00 and 18.00–23.00, closed Sun

 Davidoff €€–€€€ International/Portuguese cuisine, with music. ⓐ Quinta Shopping, Quinta do Lago ☎ 289 39 24 23

 Iberico €€–€€€ Good food in elegant surroundings in this popular Portuguese restaurant. ⓐ Almancil (Vale do Lobo road) ☎ 289 39 40 66 🕐 Open 18.00–22.30 ❶ Reservations essential

Julia's 1 €€–€€€ The best place for beach-side drinks and dining, Julia's is renowned for its excellent seafood and secret-recipe African rice. ⓐ The original is at Praia do Garrão; its younger sister, **Julia's 2** (Barca Velha), is on the beach at Vale do Lobo ☎ 289 39 65 12 (Julia's 1); 289 39 39 39, ext 5416 (Julia's 2) 🕐 Both open 10.00–midnight

 **Memories of China** €€€ Ken Lo's famous Chinese restaurant. Try the sizzling three-seafood platter. ⓐ David Lloyd Tennis Centre, Vale do Lobo 🕐 Open 18.00–midnight

Mr Freddie's €€–€€€ The menu is a cut above the average: beef tenderloin with Dao wine, pork filet with apples and honey, rack of lamb with mustard and rosemary. Dine indoors or on the tree-shaded terrace. ⓐ Val do Lobo–Almancil road ⓣ 289 39 36 51

Pig and Whistle €€–€€€ No, this is not yet another Brit-pub but a smart family-run restaurant and bar, known throughout the region for its first-class international cooking. ⓐ Old EN 125, Almancil ⓣ 289 39 52 16 ⓛ Open Mon–Sat 18.30–late, closed Sun

Pizza Pasta Fantasia €€ Italian pizza and fresh pasta dishes. ⓐ Buganvilia Placa 15, Quinta do Lago ⓣ 289 39 40 80

Tarantino's €€–€€€ Chefs from Milan work wonders with the abundance of local fresh vegetables and seafood, serving *osso buco*, sage-scented veal and dilled sea bass. The tranquil dining room is the perfect setting for the food. ⓐ Quinta Shopping, Quinta do Lago ⓣ 289 39 23 95 ⓔ tarantino@mail.telepac.pt

The Teapot €–€€ Nice spot for a traditional afternoon cuppa, with a pretty garden terrace in which to relax. Also serves lunches, including a Sunday roast. ⓐ Almancil ⓣ 289 39 36 25 ⓛ Open Tues–Sun 11.00–18.00, closed Mon

SHOPPING

 Apolonia Supermarket Well-stocked English-style supermarket with a good selection of wines and spirits. ⓐ Rua 5 de Outubro, Almancil

Florida Golf All the kit you'll need. ⓐ Rua 5 de Outubro, Almancil

Griffin Bookshop English-language fiction and non-fiction, second-hand and children's books, plus ordering service. ⓐ Rua 5 de Outubro 206-A, Almancil ⓣ 289 39 39 04

Monte Gordo
endless beach

People think 'big' in Monte Gordo: the beach is vast; the hotels and apartments are in high-rise blocks, and – for the big spenders visiting the town – there is a casino on the promenade. Popular with Spanish families, who cross the border to enjoy the lower prices, Monte Gordo is a lively resort with disco-clubs, karaoke bars and restaurants offering folk dancing and *fado* evenings.

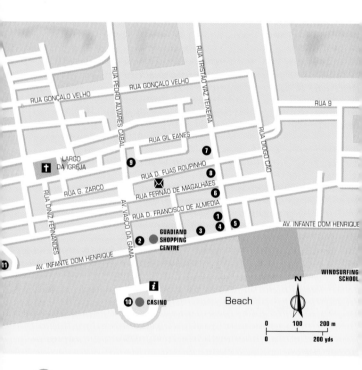

The main reason for coming to Monte Gordo has to be the beach – 20 km (12.5 miles) of shimmering sand, backed by pine forests and citrus orchards, and stretching as far as Praia Verde, Alagoa and Manta Rota. For water sports enthusiasts, the off-shore lagoons are perfect for sailing, water skiing and windsurfing, while the sea-water temperatures here are the highest in Portugal.

The stately 18th-century town of **Vila Real de Santo António**, only 3 km (1.8 miles) away, makes a pleasant change from sea and sand. It was laid out on a grid plan by the Marquês de Pombal, famous for redesigning Lisbon after the Great Earthquake of 1755. Most visitors stop for lunch (shellfish is the local speciality) before making the short border crossing to Spain. The road bridge linking Vila Real de Santo António to its Spanish counterpart, **Ayamonte**, was completed in 1991. Alternatively, you can make the journey by ferry. There are crossings at 40-minute intervals.

Not everything in Monte Gordo is modern – take a tour of the town in an old-fashioned pony and trap, leaving from the sea front by the Hotel Vasco da Gama (summer afternoons only).

THINGS TO SEE & DO
Cycling ★
Explore the town and local area by bicycle. You can rent bikes from **Fernandos** at daily or weekly rates. ⓐ Guadiana Shopping Centre, Avenida Infante Dom Henrique ⓘ 281 51 38 81

Jeep safaris ★
Join in a one-day jeep convoy and explore the inland region. Ask at the tourist office for further details.

Sea fishing ★
The Blue Emerald – a 33-footer – takes beginners and experienced anglers on deep-sea and big-game fishing trips. Ask the tourist office for details.

SHOPPING

 The shops in the Guadiana Shopping Centre and on Avenida Infante Dom Henrique in Monte Gordo cater for most visitors' needs.

Carvela Nice pottery and glassware, locally made candles and mugs.

Marrachino Supermarket with an excellent range of port, as well as fresh bread.

Other places in Monte Gorde, include:

Casa Caravela Good selection of crystal. ❸ Rua Dr Teófilo Braga, Vila Real de Santo António

Sol Dorado This interesting shop has a wide range of colourful local needlework and handicrafts. ❸ Rua Dr Téofilo Braga 18, Vila Real

Ourivesaria Portuguese jewellery, gold and silverware.
❸ Rua Dr Teófilo Braga, Vila Real de Santo António

RESTAURANTS & BARS (see map on page 52)

A Cabana €€ ❶ The speciality of this steak-house is shrimps in a spicy sauce, and, of course, outstanding beef. ❸ Rua Bartolomeu Perestrelo ❶ 281 51 18 45 🕒 Open noon–late

Copacabana €€–€€€ ❷ Swordfish steaks, sardines, pork kebabs, etc are grilled on a huge barbecue in the courtyard of this promenade restaurant. ❸ Avenida Infante Dom Henrique ❶ 281 54 15 36 🕒 Open 11.00–midnight

O Dourado €€ ❸ This restaurant, with a shady beach terrace, offers a wide range of traditional Portuguese dishes. Its speciality is a whole range of *cataplanas*. ❸ Avenida Infante Dom Henrique ❶ 281 51 22 02 🕒 Open 10.00–late

Goa €€ **4** An Indian restaurant with a difference. For the uninitiated, a supplementary menu explains the ingredients that provide the distinctive Goan taste. ⓐ Rua Fernando Pó ⓣ 281 51 26 06 ⓛ Open 18.00–late

Ipanema €–€€ **5** Home-baked baguettes, cakes, pastries and ice creams served under straw beach parasols. ⓐ Avenida Infante Dom Henrique ⓛ Open 10.00–late

Mr Bee's €–€€ **6** Snug British bar-restaurant serving traditional British home cooking in a friendly atmosphere. ⓐ Rua Tres ⓛ Open 10.00–late

Pizzeria La Mamma €€ **7** A busy Italian restaurant in the centre of town, offering excellent salads and pasta dishes as well the usual variety of pizzas. ⓐ Rua Tristão Vaz Teixeira ⓣ 281 54 28 65 ⓛ Open 11.00–late

Rendezvous € **8** Diners eat to the accompaniment of pop or *fado* music in this friendly Anglo-Portuguese bar-restaurant. Dishes include favourites such as vegetable or steak pie with chips, chicken *piri-piri* and lasagne. ⓐ Rua Tristão Vaz Teixeria ⓣ 281 54 25 69 ⓛ Open 10.00–23.00

Restaurant Bar Swiss € **9** Attractive dining room and patio with good-value food. ⓐ Rua Alvares Cabal 37 ⓣ 281 54 43 60

NIGHTLIFE
Casino de Monte Gordo **10** The newest casino in the Algarve, with gaming rooms, floor show and restaurant. ⓣ 281 51 22 24

Paddy's Irish Bar €–€€ **11** Lively karaoke bar. ⓐ Avenida Infante Dom Henrique ⓛ Open 20.00–late, happy hour 20.00–22.00

Montechoro & 'the Strip'
bright lights and beaches

The inexorable spread upwards and outwards of what was originally the small fishing village of Albufeira has spawned the satellite resorts of what has been christened Nova Albufeira (New Albufeira).

Just a couple of kilometres (1.2 miles) east of Albufeira Old Town, perched on the top of a hill, stands the resort of Montechoro, dominated by the landmark Hotel Montechoro. From here, the long, straight Avenida Sá Carneiro (known to everyone as 'the Strip'), lined with bars, restaurants and souvenir shops, descends all the way to the lovely, if often crowded, beach of Praia da Oura. At the crossroads, around halfway down the Strip, the area's name changes from Montechoro to Areais de São João.

BEACHES
East of **Praia da Oura** are the small beaches of **Balaia** and the charming beach cove of **Olhos d'Agua** (literally 'Eyes of Water'), so named for its rock formations. **Açoteias** is a small pine-shaded village next to the splendid golden 2 km (1.2 mile) long beach of **Praia da Falésia**, backed by the eastern-most cliffs in the Algarve.

Walk into Albufeira along the cliffs from Praia da Oura. It's a lovely scenic walk. Time it to arrive at sunset, then you can enjoy the pretty sight of Albufeira's fairy-lit central market stalls.

SHOPPING
If you are self-catering, there's the **Marrachino** supermarket at the crossroads on the Strip, but for more choice go to the large **Modelo** supermarket on the main road to Albufeira. For local colour, continue on the same road to Albufeira's fruit, vegetable and fish market (mornings only).

🔺 *The popular beach of Praia da Oura*

RESTAURANTS

O Antonio €€ Local foods, sensibly priced, make this a popular spot for locals and holiday makers. Fresh fish, steaks and their famous prawns in garlic highlight the menu. ⓐ Estrada das Acoteias ⓣ 289 50 26 83 🕔 Open from 18.00

Le Bistro €€–€€€ French-inspired dishes are beautifully presented in a serene setting, with a terrace surrounded by palm trees. The children's menu is also well above the ordinary. ⓐ Rua Almeida Garret 30 ⓣ 289 51 21 30 ⓔ le.bistro@iol.pt 🕔 Open Tues–Sun eves

A Lagosteira €€ Traditional, long-established seafood restaurant with a great outdoor eating area, sometimes with live music. Good for families. ⓐ Aldeia das Açoteias, just past the Sheraton Hotel ⓣ 289 50 16 79 🕔 Open 11.00–midnight

Hollandaide €–€€ Restaurant catering for families, with a kids' menu and nappy-changing facilities. ⓐ Areias S João, Avenida Dos Descobermentos ⓣ 289 56 13 24 🕔 Open Mon–Sat from 10.00

O Poente €€ Smart, traditional restaurant. Grills are the speciality. ⓐ Brejos-Montechoro, 1 km (0.6 miles) behind Hotel Montechoro on road to N 125 (by Repsol garage) ⓣ 289 54 14 19 🕔 Open 11.00–23.00

🍴 **Puccini's** €€–€€€ Pizzas and Italian favourites are available to take away or to enjoy in the easy ambiance of the dining room or large terrace. Live music and daily specials keep people coming back. ⓐ Montechoro Parque ⓣ 289 58 64 72 ⓦ www.montechoropark.com

🍴 **Tem Avonde** €–€€ Small restaurant with local dishes, changing daily, plus children's menu. ⓐ Rua Mouzinho Albuquerque, Montechoro ⓣ 969 03 76 69 ⓔ temavonde@portugal-info.net

🍴 **Valentines Bistro** €–€€ Family-run restaurant with good prices and an enclosed dining area where children can roam safely. The extensive menu has something to please any taste at breakfast, lunch or dinner. ⓐ Avenida Sa Carneiro ⓣ 289 54 15 66

NIGHTLIFE

Erin's Isle Popular Irish bar and restaurant with live music in the beer garden and air-conditioned bar. ⓐ Montechoro Parque, the Strip ⓣ 289 54 29 49 ⓛ Open 09.30–late ⓘ Kids' play area (20.30–00.30)

Kiss Disco The Algarve's most famous and buzzing disco with regular theme nights. Entrance charge includes one free drink. ⓐ Rua Vasco da Gama, the Strip ⓛ Open 23.00–06.00

Restaurant Bar Reno's Pleasant bar serving well-prepared local dishes, with music. ⓐ The Strip (Areias S João) ⓣ 289 51 30 74

> ## MONTECHORO PARQUE
> Next to the Hotel Montechoro, this buzzing courtyard comprises several eating and drinking establishments. These include **A Palmeira** (drinks and snacks), **Rovers Return** (pub), **Dona Graciela** (international/Italian dishes), **Bulgari** (a steak-house), **Monte China** (Chinese food) and a laundry. There's also **Maxi-Mini Golf**.

Sagres & Cape St Vincent

The small fishing port of Sagres (pronounced 'Sah-gresh') lies just a few kilometres from Cape St Vincent, where the fierce westerly winds sweep in from the Atlantic, sending the sea crashing against the rocks. It's an area of stunning natural beauty, with pristine, surf-washed beaches backed by towering cliffs and dunes. Apart from water sports, visitors can look forward to bracing coastal walks, fishing trips, boat trips and jeep safaris.

Standing on Sagres Point, a bleak promontory to the west of the town, is the *fortaleza* (fortress). It was built in the 15th century and its forbidding grey walls once contained Henry the Navigator's famous school of seamanship. From here there are several ways to reach the Cape: by boat (cruises leave from the fishing harbour), by car (via the EN 268) or on foot – the cliff-top walk is exhilarating, with fabulous views along the coast and out to sea.

On the way is another fortress, the 17th-century Fortaleza do Beliche, restored in the 1960s. Cape St Vincent, mainland Europe's most south westerly point, was 'the end of the world' until Vasco da Gama, Magellan and other Portuguese explorers opened up the maritime routes to Africa and America. From the top of the lighthouse it's a 60 m (200 ft) drop to the hazardous rocks below. The souvenir stalls at the Cape do a brisk trade in chunky, hand-knitted fishermen's sweaters.

Watching the sun set over the Cape is an unforgettable experience whatever the time of year, but in spring and autumn, there's the added pleasure of seeing huge numbers of migrating birds winging their way over the cliffs.

◐ *Dramatic cliffs at Cape St Vincent*

THINGS TO SEE & DO

Boat trips ★★★

Boats depart daily for Cape St Vincent and magnificent views of the windswept Costa Vicentina. The round trip takes approximately two hours. Fishing excursions (first-timers and experienced anglers welcome), including shark fishing, are also on offer, usually departing daily at 16.30 hours – the round trip takes approximately three hours. Catches include sea bass, bream, squid and mackerel. Ground fishing is also available if you give at least 48 hours' notice. Contact **Turinfo** (🕐 282 62 48 73) for details of all boat trips.

Fortaleza ★★

Only the chapel and the castle walls survive from the small town built here by Henry the Navigator. Climb the battlements for superb views of the Cape, then take a look at the Rosa do Ventos (Wind Rose), a stone dial 43 m (47 yd) in diameter, thought to have served as a mariner's compass.

Fortaleza do Beliche ★★

Overlooking the sea is an attractive, white-domed chapel dedicated to St Catherine. The original fortress was destroyed by Sir Francis Drake in 1587 in an operation designed to forestall the Spanish Armada.

Lighthouse ★★

Visitors may be allowed to climb the tower to inspect the twin 1000 watt lamps, visible for up to 90 km (56 miles) and among the most powerful in Europe. Up to 200 ships navigate the busy shipping lanes every day. Opening times are at the discretion of the lighthouse keepers.

BEACHES

There are four good beaches near Sagres. The largest and most sheltered is **Praia do Martinhal**, near **Baleeira** and the Windsurfing Club. Closer to the village is **Praia da Mareta**. **Praia do Tonel** is good for surfing, while **Praia do Beliche** is an excellent sandy beach, but is vulnerable to strong westerlies. Sailboards and mountain bikes can be rented.

THE COSTA VICENTINA
Jeep safari convoys head for the beautiful, unspoilt west coast
(contact **Turinfo** ❷ Praça da República, Sagres ❶ 282 62 00 03).
Many of the magnificent beaches, backed by dunes and sheer
cliffs, are accessible by car. Take the EN 268 from Sagres to Vila do
Bispo and the left turning to Praia do Castelejo, where the moors
behind the cliffs are covered in wild flowers.

Alternatively, continue along the main road to the tiny village of
Carrapateira and the nearby beaches of Amado and (perhaps the
most spectacular of all) Bordeira.

RESTAURANTS

O Batedor €€ Excellent seafront location and varied menu,
including peppered steak, grilled sardines and Portuguese steak.
❷ Avenida das Naus, Baleeira ❶ 282 92 48 10 ❹ Open 08.00–late

Bossa Nova €€ Friendly restaurant with terrace –serves pizza,
pasta, vegetarian, meat and seafood dishes. Children's menu.
❷ Rua da Mareta, Sagres ❶ 282 62 42 19 ❹ Open noon–midnight

Fortaleza do Beliche €€–€€€ Charming dining room in the
fortress, serving updated regional dishes. Seafood is a speciality.
The views are stunning, as the fortress sits on a cliff overhanging the
sea. ❷ Estrada Cabo Sao Vicente ❶ 282 62 42 25

O Pescador €€–€€€ Quality seafood restaurant specializing in
Portuguese dishes, such as *cataplana* and grilled swordfish. ❷ Rua
Comandante Matoso, Baleeira ❶ 282 62 41 92 ❹ Open 08.00–22.00

NIGHTLIFE

Topas Disco in the centre of town playing live rock and pop all night.
❷ Near the Parque de Campismo ❹ Open 23.00–06.00

COMMERCIAL HARBOUR

MARKET

PRAÇA GIL EANES

PRAÇA LUIS DE CAMÕES

COASTAL EXCURSIONS

FERRY TO MEIA PRAIA BEACH

Meia Praia Beach

PRAÇA INFANTE DON HENRIQUE

SANTO ANTÓNIO

LARGO VASCO GARCIA

BOATS TO GROTTOES

FORTE PONTA DA BANDEIRA

Town Beach

OTHER BEACHES

1	TOWN HALL
2	STATUE OF KING SEBASTIÃO
3	RUA ALFONSO DA ALMA
4	FORMER SLAVE MARKET
5	STATUE OF HENRY THE NAVIGATOR
6	GOVERNOR'S CASTLE
7	MUSEU MUNICIPAL

0   100   200 m
0   200 yds

RUA VICTOR DA COSTA SILVA
RUA VASCO DA GAMA
RUA X CRISODOMO DOS SANTOS
RUA DA CAPELINHA
AV. DOS DESCOBRIMENTOS
RUA DON JOAQUIM MACHADO
RUA PORTA DE PORTUGAL
RUA JOGO DA BOLA
RUA 25 DE ABRIL
RUA DA BARROCA
AV. DOS DESCOBRIMENTOS
RUA INFANTE DE SAGRES
RUA MARREIROS NETO
RUA CANDIDO DOS REIS
RUA S. LOPES
RUA PROFESSOR LUIS DE AZEVEDO
RUA D. CASTRO DOS GOVERNADORES
RUA GIL VICENTE
RUA LANCAROTE DE FREITAS
RUA DE S. GONÇALO
RUA GEN. ALBERTO DE SILVEIRA
RUA DO JARDIM
RUA CARDEAL NETO
RUA DR. MENDONÇA
RUA MIGUEL BOMBARDA
RUA SAN JOSE
N125

Lagos
harbour, fortress and beaches

Lagos (pronounced 'Lah-gosh') is an attractive town with a colourful past and plenty of good restaurants, shops, churches and museums.

The most famous former resident of Lagos, Henry the Navigator, is commemorated by a statue in Praça Infante Dom Henrique. In the corner of the square is an arcaded building where African slaves were once bought and sold; it is now used for art exhibitions. The massive gateway at the bottom of Rua Miguel Bombarda forms part of the city walls, dating from the 14th to 16th centuries, while the rooftop of the Forte Ponta da Bandeira (now a museum) affords excellent views of the superb natural harbour. Prettily painted houses and cobbled courtyards characterize the area around Rua da Barroca, where restaurants also cluster. Praça Gil Eanes contains a monument to King Sebastião, who was killed on an ill-fated crusading expedition to Morocco in 1578. Around the square is an extensive pedestrian precinct with bars, cafés and shops selling eye-catching local handicrafts and souvenirs.

THINGS TO SEE & DO
Forte Ponta da Bandeira (Flag Point Fort) ★
This tiny 17th-century fort houses some archaeological finds, a small exhibition (in Portuguese only) on the Age of Discoveries, a chapel dedicated to St Barbara and the **Taverna** restaurant. ❶ 282 76 14 10 ❷ Open Tues–Sun 09.30–noon and 14.00–17.00, closed Mon ❶ Admission charge

Museu Municipal (Municipal Museum) ★★
Set behind the famous church of Santo António, this overlooked museum is an old-fashioned cabinet of curiosities, including church and archaeological treasures, animal fetuses in formaldehyde and a bizarre five-legged calf. ❸ Rua General Alberto de Silveira ❶ 282 76 23 01 ❷ Open Tues–Sun 09.30–12.30 and 14.00–17.00, closed Mon and public holidays ❶ Small admission charge

Ponta da Piedade (Piety Point) ★★★

Boat trips depart from the Forte Ponta da Bandeira to visit these extraordinary marine grottoes. The sunsets are spectacular, and scuba diving is available (see page 106). Ask at the tourist office for further details.

Santo António ★★★

The lavishly decorated 'golden' chapel is one of the few to survive the earthquake of 1755. Coloured *azulejo* tiles decorate the lower walls of the baroque chapel; the remainder is covered with fantastic ornamental woodcarving and giltwork. ❸ Rua General Alberto de Silveira ◐ Open Tues–Sun 09.00–12.30 and 14.00–17.00, closed Mon and public holidays

RESTAURANTS & BARS (see map on page 64)

On Rua Alfonso da Almeida ❶ there is a row of traditional Portuguese restaurants, including **Chicken Piri Piri**, **O Cantinho Algarvio** and **Pouso d'Infante**. All are good, mid-priced places to sample authentic cooking.

Casa Amarela €–€€ ❷ Wicker chairs and glass tables beckon tired shoppers in for a very civilized cuppa at this quiet tearoom. ⓐ Rua 25 de Abril ◐ Open Mon–Sat 10.00–midnight, Sun 10.00–15.00

Dom Henrique €–€€ ❸ Watch the chefs create dinner in the open kitchen. Traditional local dishes and international favourites fill the well-planned menu. ⓐ Rua 25 de Abril 75 ✆ 282 76 35 63

Dom Sebastião €€€ ❹ Probably the town's most celebrated (and touristy) restaurant. Fish and shellfish are the specialities. Opt for a romantic evening inside rather than lunch outside. ⓐ Rua 25 de Abril ✆ 282 76 27 95 ◐ Open 11.00–15.00 and 18.30–22.30

A Floresta €€ ❺ A warm, family-owned restaurant whose generous servings make it a repeat favourite for many visitors. The excellent salads are especially welcome. ❸ Rua Antonio Crisogono dos Santos ✆ 282 76 37 19 ◐ Open 11.00–midnight

SHOPPING

Olaria Nova Features some of the best modern pottery in the Algarve, with many inventive contemporary designs. It also includes some lovely traditional and ethnic clothing, shoes, accessories and jewellery. ❸ Rua 25 de Abril

Casa de Papagaio Named after its resident parrots, is a fascinating Aladdin's cave of architectural salvage (including large church Madonnas and cherubs) and second-hand bits and bobs. ❸ Rua 25 de Abril)

Fools and Horses € ❻ English bar and restaurant with a good value menu. British draught beers are on sale. Karaoke and quiz nights. Sky Sports TV. ❸ Rua Barbosa Viana 7 ❶ 282 76 29 70 ● Open Mon–Sat 10.00–15.00 and 18.00–02.00, Sun 18.00–02.00

Mediterraneo €€ ❼ The most inventive and interesting menu in Lagos. Vegetarians and vegans are well catered for in this friendly restaurant with a large terrace for alfresco dining. ❸ Rua da Senhora da Graça ❶ 282 76 84 76 ● Open Tues–Sat 18.00–23.00

NIGHTLIFE

Most of the conspicuous drinking in Lagos is done at the end of Rua 25 de Abril, where half a dozen bars cluster. Look up to see the most attractive of them all, **Bon Vivant**, with a Gaudí-inspired interior.

Ferradura Excellent locals' bar run by a very friendly Portuguese owner who speaks perfect English. Cheap beer and good *petiscos* (snacks). ❸ Rua 1 de Maio 26A ● Open Mon–Sat 11.00–late

Stevie Roy's This celebrated jazz club lays on live blues and jazz on Saturday nights. ❸ Rua de Sra da Graca 9 ❶ 282 92 38 83 ● Open 20.00–04.00

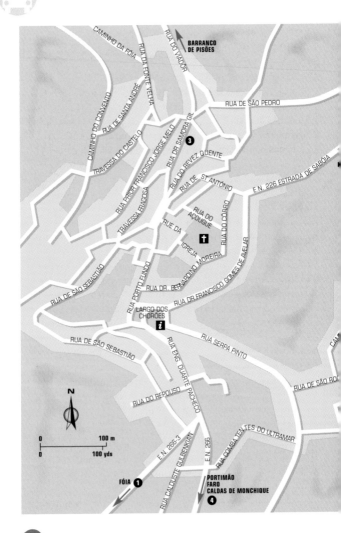

Monchique
hill village and spa

The village of Monchique (pronounced 'Mon-sheek') lies at the heart of the Serra de Monchique mountain range. Its narrow cobbled streets climb steeply, and are lined by traditional houses painted pastel shades of pink, blue and green, with old-fashioned gas lamps protruding here and there from the upper storeys. The Serra is also famous for its restaurants specializing in barbecue lunches of spicy chicken *piri-piri*.

THINGS TO SEE & DO
Caldas de Monchique ★★

Caldas is famous for its hot springs, long believed to have curative and health-giving properties. It is a lovely little village lying on the edge of a densely wooded ravine, perfect for walking. The spa is still functioning, and (if you can stomach it) you can sample the original sulphurous spa water. Better known, and much more palatable, is the water bottled in the village and sold all over the Algarve. For something stronger, try *medronho*, the local liqueur made from the berries of the arbutus, or strawberry trees, that grow locally.

Fóia ★★

At just over 900 m (3000 ft), Fóia is the highest point in the Algarve. There are spectacular views of the coast, from Cape St Vincent in the west, to Vilamoura in the east. On a clear day, there are views across the rocky plateaux to terraced hillsides planted with eucalyptus, arbutus and cork oaks – sometimes even to the mountain ranges south of Lisbon.

Serious walkers should get hold of a copy of the *Trilhos de Bio-Park Network Monchique* map. It covers 300 km (188 miles) of trails that are suitable for walking and mountain biking, all in Ordnance Survey detail. Another invaluable aid to serious walkers is *Landscapes of the Algarve* published by Sunflower Books. Both are on sale locally.

RESTAURANTS (see map on page 68)

Abrigo da Montanha €€ **①** A spacious dining room in a mountain lodge, where open fireplaces add to the cosy, rustic atmosphere. The genial hosts and staff add to the experience, serving imaginative renditions of traditional Portuguese dishes. **ⓐ** Estrada Foia **ⓣ** 282 91 21 31 **ⓦ** www.abrigodamontanha.com

Bica-Boa €€ **②** A traditional inn that has been restored by its Irish-Portuguese owners. There is a wide range of regional and international dishes on offer, which can be enjoyed in the dining room or on the outside terrace. **ⓐ** Estrada de Lisboa **ⓣ** 282 91 22 71 **ⓛ** Open 10.00–midnight

SHOPPING

Casa do Forno Typical Algarvian souvenirs and crafts. **ⓐ** Rua Dr Francisco Gomes de Avelar, Monchique

Casa da Praça Some more unusual handicrafts and souvenirs, and an ideal starting point to look for that elusive gift. **ⓐ** Praça Alexandre Herculano, Monchique

O Descansa Pernas Portuguese *artesanato* (handicraft shop) specializing in cork, pottery, leatherware and souvenir ornaments. **ⓐ** Estrada de Sabóia, Monchique

O Poço Beautiful cork ornaments; also hand-decorated pottery. The shop is on the road to Fóia. **ⓐ** Estrada da Fóia

Ardecor The place for high-quality handicrafts, clothing and accessories, wooden toys, pottery and lovely hand-painted wooden furniture. **ⓐ** Largo dos Chorões (opposite main square), Monchique

And… thick winter woollies may be the last thing on your mind while you are down on the sunbaked coast, but it's cool and windy at Fóia, and good-quality, hand-knitted cardigans and pullovers are always on sale here.

A Charrete €–€€ ❸ Old wagon wheels are part of the decor in this attractive and friendly local restaurant. There's a reasonably priced tourist menu as well as the wide selection of regional specialities on offer. ⓐ Rua Dr Samora Gil, Monchique ❶ 282 91 21 42 🕒 Open 10.00–22.00

Jardim das Oliveiras €€–€€€ ❶ A lovely restaurant in a charming rustic setting just off the main road to Fóia. Chicken *piri-piri*, snails and hearty local meat dishes are the speciality. ⓐ Sitio do Porto Escuro, Monchique ❶ 282 91 28 74 🕒 Open 10.00–late

Paraiso da Montanha € ❶ Inexpensive regional cooking, including excellent chicken *piri-piri*. The restaurant is on the road to Fóia. ⓐ Estrada da Fóia ❶ 282 91 21 50 🕒 Open 10.00–midnight

Quinta de São Bento €€€ ❶ The perfect place to celebrate a special occasion, this traditional Portuguese restaurant has won several international awards and was once the summer residence of the Portuguese Royal House of Bragança. Just as impressive are the views from the restaurant's vantage point at nearly 900 m (3000 ft). ⓐ Quinta São Bento, Estrada da Fóia (about 5 km/3 miles from town) ❶ 282 91 21 43 🕒 Open noon–late

Rampa €–€€ ❶ Simple country restaurant with wonderful mountain views. While taking them in, tuck into the tasty, home-made soup, followed by chicken *piri-piri* (the best in town) and their delicious almond cake. ⓐ Estrada da Fóia, Samargal ❶ 282 91 28 74 🕒 Open 11.00–late

Rouxinol €€–€€€ ❹ The Scandinavian-run 'Nightingale' is set in a delightful rustic hunting lodge and offers fondues, game (in season) and a good vegetarian choice. It's also open for coffee, snacks and home-made cakes. ⓐ Estrada de Monchique (opposite turning to Caldas de Monchique) ❶ 282 91 39 75 🕒 Open noon–22.00

Portimão
shopping and sardines

A busy port on the River Arade, Portimão is also the Algarve's largest shopping centre. Wander around the town's main squares, where many of its 19th-century houses have painted tile facades and fine, wrought-iron balconies, or take a boat trip up the river or along this picturesque section of the Algarve coast.

THINGS TO SEE & DO
Arade Cruise ★★

Take a trip up the River Arade aboard an old-fashioned Portuguese 'gondola' (a traditional, brightly painted, high-prowed vessel – nothing like the Venetian type!) to the beautiful town of Silves (see page 74).

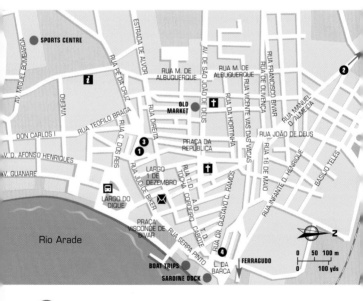

Boat trips ★★

A half-day trip will head east past the glorious beach coves near Carvoeiro, which host a curiosity of old sea caves with dramatic arches and grottoes, and nearby towering rock formations.

Ferragudo ★★

On the opposite side of the estuary, this quaint village has typically Portuguese architecture with a strong Moorish influence. Just beyond the village is the *fortaleza* (fortress), not open to the public, on the excellent beach of Praia Grande.

RESTAURANTS & BARS (see map opposite)

The charming, flower-filled **Largo da Barca**, reached by walking underneath the arches of the Sardine Dock, is home to Portimão's best seafood restaurants. **Forte & Feio** (📞 282 41 88 94), **Dona Barca** (📞 282 48 41 89) and the highly rated **Trinca Espinhas** (📞 282 41 88 54).

Blarney Castle €–€€ ❶ Portimão's liveliest bar – Irish, of course, with a good selection of draught beers. Live music nightly, and a Western-style menu. 🏠 Rua Damião L Faria e Castro 📞 282 41 42 40 🕐 Open 10.30–late

O Buque €–€€ ❷ Watch the chefs transform impeccably fresh seafood into dinner here, in beautiful surroundings. 🏠 EN 125, Parchal, 2 km (1.2 miles) from town 📞 282 42 46 78 🕐 Closed Sun

Kibom €€ ❸ A typical, one-storey Algarve house specializing in fish and shellfish. 🏠 Rua Damião L Faria e Castro 📞 282 41 46 23 🕐 Open 11.00–16.00 and 18.00–23.00

A Ribeirinha €–€€ ❹ This tiny café on a side street near Largo da Barca is a favourite with locals for its fresh meat and seafood. Nothing fancy. 🏠 Rua da Barca 15 📞 282 41 47 30 🕐 Open Mon–Sat 10.00–15.00 and 18.00–midnight

Silves
ancient Moorish capital

Modern visitors to Silves (pronounced 'Sil-vesh') will find it hard to believe that this sleepy town was once the wealthy capital of a Moorish province. When the Arabs were finally expelled in 1242, the Christians returned, remodelling the castle and replacing the mosque with a cathedral. Today Silves is the centre of a prosperous farming region, the pretty, unspoilt villages surrounded by orchards producing oranges, lemons, figs and other fruit in abundance.

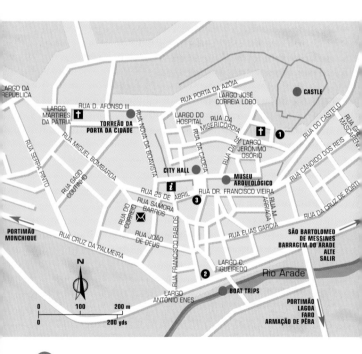

THINGS TO SEE & DO

Arade boat trips ★★

Take an old-fashioned Portuguese 'gondola' on a 90-minute trip to Portimão (see page 72), along the River Arade, which was once the highway that brought fabulous riches to Silves. ☎ 282 42 42 43 for reservations and details ⏰ Trips Mon–Sat.

Castle ★★★

The network of 13th-century battlements and turrets is still largely intact, though heavily restored. From the parapets the views of the Arade Valley are spectacular. In the flower-filled castle courtyard are traces of an Arab palace, built by the last Moorish ruler of Silves. The courtyard is said to be haunted by an enchanted Moorish girl. This sylph-like figure is said to appear at midnight on Midsummer's Eve as she awaits the handsome prince who will one day break her spell. ⏰ Open 09.00–18.00 ❶ Admission charge

Cathedral ★

Like the castle, Silves Cathedral dates from the 13th century and, despite a subsequent baroque facelift, the rib-vaulted choir and tombs of crusading knights are reminders of its medieval origins. ⏰ Open 08.30–18.30 (in summer); winter times vary ❶ Donation expected

Fábrica do Inglês (The Englishman's Factory) ★

The 19th-century English cork factory has been converted into a museum with its own brewery and six restaurants. Every night at 23.00 a street party with music and clowns is staged featuring *Aquavision* – a spectacular multimedia water and laser show. ☎ 282 44 04 40 ❶ Admission is free until 18.00

Horse riding ★

Go trekking through some of the most beautiful countryside in the Algarve. Beginners and experienced riders welcome. ➌ Vale Fuzeiros (near Messines) ☎ 282 33 24 66

Museu Arqueológico (Archaeological Museum) ★★

The museum, constructed around a 12th-century Arab well, has Bronze Age, Roman and Moorish items. ⓐ Rua das Portas de Loulé ⓛ Open Mon–Sat 09.00–18.00 ⓘ Admission charge

Torreão da Porta da Cidade (Turret of the City Gate) ★★

This barbican is the last surviving inner city wall gate. It was built in the 12th or 13th century and for many centuries was home to the municipal council. Today it holds the municipal library. ⓛ Open Tues–Sat 09.30–13.00 and 14.00–17.30 ⓘ Admission free

Alte ★★★

Alte is one of the prettiest villages in Portugal, with balconies wreathed in oleander, hibiscus and geraniums, and a striking 16th-century church. Alte is renowned for its singing and folk dancing ensembles. ⓘ 282 47 86 66 (Alte tourist office) for more details

---

SHOPPING

Housed in a lovely 16th-century building near the castle is the **Estúdio Destra**, the studio and gallery of Kate Swift, an artist renowned for her hand-painted tiles and ceramics.

RESTAURANTS (see map on page 74)

Café Inglês €€ ❶ This Anglo-Portuguese venture, located in a charming old town house, has a perfect setting on the steps of the castle next to the cathedral, with everything from full Portuguese meals to coffee and delicious, home-made cakes. ⓘ 282 44 25 85 ⓛ Open Mon 09.30–18.00, Tues–Fri 09.30–22.00 and Sat 18.00–22.00

O Cais €€ ❷ Riverside restaurant with traditional Algarvian decor, specializing in charcoal-grilled dishes, especially fish. ⓐ Rua José Estevão ⓘ 282 44 52 02 ⓛ Open for lunch and dinner

Casa Velha de Silves €€ ❸ Traditional Portuguese restaurant overlooking the main square, serving full meals, omelettes and sandwiches. Regular *fado* and other folk music events in the basement bar. ⓐ Rua 25 de Abril ❶ 282 44 54 91 ❶ Open 11.00–15.00 and 18.00–23.00

◐ *Relaxed, open-air eating*

Faro
Algarve's capital

The capital of the Algarve, Faro (pronounced 'Fah-roh'), is a lively commercial centre and port with an authentic Portuguese atmosphere. There is half a day's sightseeing in the relaxed and peaceful Old Town, entered through the Arco da Vila, an imposing Italianate gateway commissioned by the bishop of Faro after the Great Earthquake of 1755 had destroyed its medieval predecessor. Beyond the arch is the spacious central square, with its cathedral and archaeological museum and streets lined with fine houses, decorated with wrought-iron balconies.

THINGS TO SEE & DO
Museu Arqueológico (Archaeological Museum) ★★
Housed in a 16th-century convent, the 1894 Archaeological Museum is the Algarve's oldest museum. The highlight of the museum is a beautiful 3rd-century AD Roman mosaic of Neptune surrounded by the four winds. ❸ Praça Alfonso III, Old Town ❼ 289 89 74 04 ● Open Mon and Sat 14.30–18.00, Tues–Fri 10.00–18.00 (May–Sept); Mon and Sat 14.00–17.30, Tues–Fri 09.30–17.30 (Oct–Apr) ❶ Admission charge

Cathedral ★
Climb the tower (68 steps) in this 13th-century building near the Archaeological Museum to enjoy great views over the town and lagoon. ❸ Old Town, Largo da Sé ● Consult tourist office for current opening hours. Church open Sundays only during services ❶ Admission free

Centro Ciência Viva (Centre of Living Science) ★
This is a hands-on discovery centre for children and adults. ● Open Tues–Sun 16.00–23.00 (July–mid-Sept); Tues–Fri 10.00–17.00 and Sat–Sun 15.00–19.00 (mid-Sept–June) ❶ Admission charge

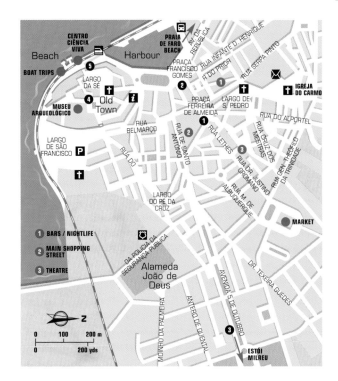

Igreja do Carmo (Carmelite Church) ★★★

Holds the macabre Capela dos Ossos, its walls lined with the bones of 1200 monks. ❸ Largo do Carmo 🕐 Open 10.00–13.00 and 15.00–17.00

Milreu ★★

These knee-high walls are all that is left of a 3rd-century Roman villa. The famous dolphin mosaics are still in reasonable condition. ❸ Signposted just before Estói 🕐 Open Tues–Sun 09.30–12.30 and 14.00–18.00 (May–Sept), closes at 17.00 in winter, closed Mon ❶ Small admission fee

Palace of Estói ★★

This charming 19th-century palace is painted pastel pink, with bright blue *azulejo* staircases, classical statues, flower-filled urns and a riot of bougainvillaea. Alas, only the gardens are open, because the building is being restored to create a hotel. ⓐ Estói village ⓒ Open Tues–Sat 09.30–12.30 and 14.00–17.30, closed Sun and Mon ❶ Admission free

RESTAURANTS & BARS (see map on page 79)

Adega Dois Irmãos €€ ❶ Since 1925 the 'Two Brothers' have been satisfying the palates of visitors and locals with superb fish and seafood. Atmospheric traditional tiled dining room. ⓐ Praça Ferreira de Almeida 25 ❶ 289 82 33 37 ⓒ Open noon–23.00

Aliança €€ ❷ This traditional Portuguese café is one of the oldest in the country. Patrons have included prime ministers as well as the French writer, Simone de Beauvoir. ⓐ Praça Francisco Gomes

Flor da Ameixa €–€€ ❸ Good value in a typical village restaurant, serving grilled sardines, sea bass (or the catch of the day), pork and chicken *piri-piri*. More exotic fare includes rabbit, partridge and roast kid. ⓐ Estoi (follow signs to Bordeira, just past the Estoi intersection) ❶ 289 99 11 16 ⓒ Open Tues–Sun 12.30–15.00 and 19.00–23.00

Piri Piri do Costa €€ ❹ This is a traditional Portuguese restaurant serving shellfish, plus grilled meat and fish dishes. ⓐ Praia de Faro ❶289 81 74 42 ⓒ Open 10.00–midnight, closed Tues

Taverna do Sé € ❺ A lovely little traditional café-bar just around the corner from the cathedral, this is the perfect place for a morning coffee and cake while listening to the sounds of classical music or jazz. ⓐ Rua do Trem, Old Town ⓒ Open 10.00–late

Tavira & Cabanas
stately town, island beaches

Tavira is an elegant town and nicely complements the growing resort of Cabanas. The coast here fragments into a series of spits, lagoons and barrier islands, which together constitute the Ria Formosa nature reserve. The warm waters on the shore side of the sandbanks are perfect for swimming, while the Atlantic beaches provide just the right conditions for windsurfing.

Get your bearings in Tavira by climbing the cobblestone lanes leading off Rua da Liberdade to the ruined **castle** (🕒 Open Mon–Fri 08.30–17.30, Sat and Sun 09.00–17.30). From the little garden within the walls there are good views of the estuary and town, and it's possible to count some of the domes and spires of Tavira's 22 churches. Next to the castle is the **Igreja de Santa Maria do Castelo** (the Church of St Mary of the Castle), remarkable for its double bell tower and enormous clock.

THINGS TO SEE & DO
Quinta da Avestruz Alegre (The Happy Ostrich Ranch) ★
See ostriches from the egg to full size. Activities for children include a mini zoo, pedal carts, bouncy castle, an assault course and crazy golf. ❶ 966 30 86 96 🕒 Open Mon–Sat 10.00–20.00 and Sun 14.00–20.00 (closes 17.00 Oct–Mar) ❶ Modest admission charge

Ria Formosa Natural Park ★★
A beautifully wild area of salt marshes and lagoons, this reserve embraces some of the best beaches in the region. Ria Formosa is also the breeding ground of many species of wading bird. The **Visitors' Centre** (📍 Quinta de Marim, 1 km/0.6 miles from Olhão on EN 125 🕒 Open 09.00–12.30 and 14.00–17.00) provides a good introduction to the area. Four-hour cycle tours of the Ria Formosa reserve are available at **Rent a Bike** ❸ Rua do Forno 33 ❶ 281 32 19 73. **Barcos do Pantanal** runs guided boat tours of the Ria Formosa, departing from Santa Luzia, west of Tavira ❶ 281 32 33 56

BEACHES

Tavira beach can be reached by ferry from the Quatro Aguas jetty between May and October. Other beaches nearby include **Pedras da Rainha**, which has its own offshore sandbank, reached by boat or on foot at low tide, and **Santa Luzia** from where there is a footbridge to Tavira Island. There is also a small railway from Pedras d'el Rei, near Santa Luzia, to **Praia de Barril** and the extensive beaches of Tavira Island.

RESTAURANTS & BARS

Cabanas:

Atmosfera € A tiny beachfront bar offering excellent English breakfasts at good value prices. ⓐ Avenida 28 Maio ⓛ Open 09.00–midnight

Copacabanas €–€€ Seafront restaurant offering grilled fish and curry, steak-on-a-stone, plus children's favourites, such as burgers, pizza and lasagne. ⓐ Avenida 28 Maio

Dona Inês €€ Large family-friendly restaurant with an attractive terrace for alfresco dining. ⓐ On the Cabanas–Tavira road ⓣ 281 37 08 01 ⓛ Open Tues–Sun 12.30–15.00 and 18.30–22.30, closed Mon

Pedros €–€€ Typical Portuguese restaurant, specializing in razor clams with beans, monkfish, *cataplana* and seafood rice. ⓐ Rua Capitão Batista Marçal 51 (by boats to beach) ⓣ 281 37 04 25

Piano Bar €€ Popular seafront restaurant serving English and international dishes. Children's menu and off-road patio. ⓐ Avenida 28 Maio 2 ⓛ Open 18.30–late, closed Sun

Tavira:

O Canecão €€ 'The world's best *cataplana*' is the boast at this shellfish specialist restaurant. ⓐ Rua José Pires Padinha 162 ⓣ 281 32 62 78 ⓛ Open noon–15.00 and 18.00–midnight, closed Thurs

Carmina € This small dining room festooned with nets and traps is full of locals when all others are empty. 🄰 Rua José Pires Padinha 96, by the fish market 🄫 281 32 22 36 🄬 Open 09.00–22.00

Imperial €–€€ An award-winning Portuguese restaurant. Try the *serrabucho de marisco* (mixed seafood with pork). 🄰 Rua José Pires Padinha 22 🄫 281 32 23 06 🄬 Open 11.00–late

Kudissanga €€ Fascinating menu of a dozen dishes from the old Portuguese colonies. Simple, tiled dining room. 🄰 Rua Dr Agusto Silva Carvalho 8 🄬 Open noon–02.00, Thurs 19.00–02.00, closed Tues

Mare's €€ Cheerful seafood restaurant on the river, directly opposite the Ilha de Tavira boat dock. *Cataplana* is their speciality. 🄰 Rua Jose Pires Padinha 134 🄫 281 31 58 15 🄬 Open 18.00–23.00

O Patio €€–€€€ Highly regarded rooftop restaurant, with an international menu and Portuguese specialities. 🄰 Rua Dr António Cabreira 30 🄫 281 32 30 08 🄬 Open 11.00–15.00 and 18.00–midnight

Patrick's €–€€ English-style pub with food, including home-made chilli, chicken *piri-piri* and various vegetarian dishes. 🄰 Rua Dr António Cabreira 🄬 Open Mon–Sat 18.00–02.00, closed Nov

Quatro Aguas €€€ Highly rated, smart, traditional fish and shellfish restaurant near the quay by the beach. 🄰 Quatro Aguas 🄫 281 32 53 29 🄬 Open Tues–Sun noon–15.30 and 18.00 and 19.00–22.30

NIGHTLIFE

Bar Toque You can find a good selection of music and cocktails here. 🄰 Rua Almirante Cândido dos Reis 118, Tavira 🄬 Open 21.00–04.00

Tavira Inn This funky, poolside jazz bar is a good bet. 🄰 Rua Chefe Antonio Alfonso 39 🄬 Open 22.30-01.00

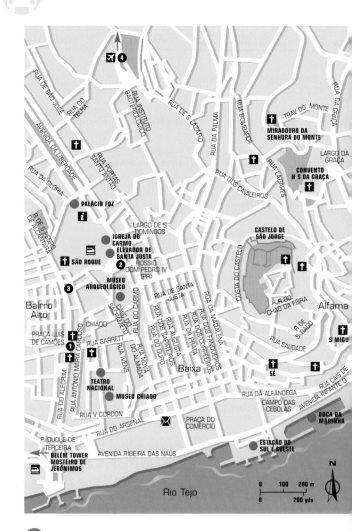

RUA DE SÃO JOSÉ

RUA DO TELHA

RUA INSTITUTO BACTERIOLÓGICO

RUA DE S LÁZARO

RUA DA PALMA

RUA BOMBARDA

TRAV DO MONTE

RUA DA GRAÇA

MIRADOURO DA SENHORA DO MONTE

AVENIDA DA LIBERDADE

RUA DA GLÓRIA

R DE S PEDRO DE ALCÂNTARA

RUA PORTAS SANTO ANTÃO

LARGO DA GRAÇA

CONVENTO N S DA GRAÇA

RUA DOS CAVALEIROS

RUA DOS LAGARES

PALÁCIO FOZ

LARGO DE S DOMINGOS

IGREJA DO CARMO

ELEVADOR DE SANTA JUSTA

ROSSIO DOM PEDRO IV (PR)

CASTELO DE SÃO JORGE

COSTA DO CASTELO

SÃO ROQUE

MUSEU ARQUEOLÓGICO

RUA DE SANTA JUSTA

CALÇ DO SACRAMENTO

RUA DO CARMO

RUA DA MADALENA

RUA DO CHÃO DA FEIRA

Alfama

Bairro Alto

RUA DA PRATA

RUA DOS CORREEIROS

RUA DOS FANQUEIROS

RUA DOS SAPATEIROS

RUA AUGUSTA

R DO

R DE S TIAGO

RUA SAUDADE

S MIGU

PRAÇA LUÍS DE CAMÕES

CHIADO

RUA GARRETT

RUA IVENS

RUA DO OURO

RUA NOVA DO ALMADA

RUA ANTÓNIO MARIA CARDOSO

RUA DO ALECRIM

Baixa

SÉ

TEATRO NACIONAL

MUSEU CHIADO

RUA V CORDON

RUA DA ALFÂNDEGA

CAMPO DAS CEBOLAS

RUA CAIS DE

AVENIDA INFANTE D

DOCA DA MARINHA

P. DUQUE DE TERCEIRA

BELÉM TOWER

MOSTEIRO DE JERÓNIMOS

RUA DO ARSENAL

PRAÇA DO COMÉRCIO

ESTAÇÃO DO SUL E SUESTE

AVENIDA RIBEIRA DAS NAUS

Rio Tejo

0   100   200 m
0   200 yds

N

Lisbon

One of the great historic capitals of Europe, Lisbon is also a port with an exciting, cosmopolitan atmosphere. Built on a series of hills at the estuary of the River Tagus, its many attractions include Castelo de São Jorge (St George's Castle), the Belém Tower and the Mosteiro de Jerónimos (Jeronimos Monastery), the medieval Alfama quarter and the restaurants and *fado* clubs of the Bairro Alto.

It is possible to see a good deal of Lisbon and to catch something of the flavour in just a few hours. South of the main square, Rossío Dom Pedro IV, is the bustling Baixa quarter. Rebuilt on a grid pattern by the Marquês de Pombal, following the Great Earthquake of 1755, each of the uniform neo-classical streets was assigned to a particular trade.

At the top of Rua do Ouro is the **Elevador de Santa Justa**, an extraordinary metal tower with a lift and viewing platform said, erroneously, to have been designed by Gustave Eiffel. Near the exit are the haunting Gothic ruins of the **Igreja do Carmo**.

An elaborate triumphal arch at the end of Rua Augusta opens out on to Praça do Comércio and the waterfront. From here, the outlook across the harbour to the statue of Cristo Rei is impressive.

Lisbon's cathedral, the **Sé** (🕐 Open 09.00–19.00), was founded in 1150 to celebrate the reconquest of the city from the Moors. An imposing Romanesque building, its twin crenellated towers give it a fortress-like appearance. The medieval tombs behind the altar commemorate prominent Portuguese noblemen.

Yellow signs point the way to the **Castelo de São Jorge** (🕐 Open 09.00–sunset), past a succession of steep, cobbled streets with washing hung out to dry on the balconies. The Moorish keep is now little more than a shell, but there are superb panoramic views of the city from the formidable battlements and walls. The courtyard has been transformed into a beautiful tree-shaded garden, the air scented with flowers, the lawns and ponds inhabited by doves, peacocks, cranes and pelicans, pheasants and (the traditional guardians of the city) ravens.

The **Mosteiro de Jerónimos** (🕒 Open Tues–Sun 10.00–17.00), one of Portugal's great religious monuments, lies a few kilometres west of Lisbon proper, in the waterfront district of Belém. Completed in 1551, the monastery has to be seen for the fantastic Manueline decoration on walls, columns and doorways: vines, creepers, wild beasts and nautical motifs.

RESTAURANTS (see map on page 84)

There are some delightful art nouveau cafés on Lisbon's main boulevard, **Avenida da Liberdade**, which runs between Rossio Dom Pedro IV and Praça do Marquês de Pombal. If you're feeling adventurous and want a more 'old world' atmosphere, head for **Alfama**, where the tiny, unpretentious restaurants specialize in fish. In the evenings, the action moves to **Bairro Alto**, a lively neighbourhood of densely packed, 17th-century houses with small, reasonably priced restaurants on almost every street corner.

Café a Brasileira €€ ❶ One of the city's most famous old-style coffee houses. ⓐ Rua Garrett 120 🕒 Open 10.00–late

O Cantinho do Aziz €€ ❷ A family-run Mozambican restaurant located just east of Rossio Dom Pedro IV, specializing in spicy meat and fish curries. ⓐ Rua de S. Lourenço 3–5 ☎ 218 87 64 72 🕒 Open Mon–Sat 11.00–midnight

Cervejaria de Trinidade €€ ❸ Nineteenth-century beer hall and restaurant, with colourful decorative tiles and high vaulted ceilings. Grilled seafood is the house speciality. ⓐ Rua Nova da Trinidade 20 ☎ 213 42 35 06 🕒 Open 10.00–midnight

Vává € ❹ A self-service cafeteria where you can eat in or take away. The choice of food includes pies, quiches, pizzas, pastries and cakes. ⓐ Avenida Estados Unidos de América 100 ☎ 217 96 67 61 🕒 Open all day

❶ *Castelo de São Jorge, Lisbon*

SHOPPING

Lisbon's lively **fish market** (🕐 Open Mon–Sat) is behind Cais do Sodré station on the waterfront. Nearby is the equally colourful **Ribeira market**, selling meat, fruit and vegetables, flowers, spices and wine. On Saturdays the famous flea market (**Feira de Ladra** – literally, 'Thieves Fair') opens early on Campo de Santa Clara in the picturesque Alfama district.

Loulé
castle, churches and crafts

A busy little town, famous for its gypsy market, Loulé (pronounced 'Loo-lay'), is also a flourishing centre of local handicrafts and one of the best places in the region to see artisans at work. Be sure to walk amongst the ruins of its 13th-century Arab castle or visit the adjacent 17th-century church.

THINGS TO SEE & DO

Castle ★★
Only the walls remain of Loulé's Arab fortress, rebuilt in the 13th century. Climb the stone steps to the battlements for fine views of the town and the surrounding countryside. ⓐ Rua Paio Perez Correia ⓛ Open Mon–Thurs 09.00–17.30 and Sat 10.00–14.00

Igreja de Nossa Senhora da Conceição ★★
Across the street from the castle is this attractive 17th-century church. The walls are decorated with blue and white tiles depicting scenes from the life of the Virgin. ⓐ Rua Paio Perez Correia ⓛ Open Mon–Fri 10.00–noon and Sat 10.00–14.00

Horse riding ★★
An exciting way to see the local countryside, with panoramic views, river crossings and sightseeing. Night rides with a barbecue are organized in the summer. Transport available. ⓐ Centro Hípico, Quinta do Azinheiro, Aldeia da Tôr ⓣ 289 41 59 91

Museu Municipal ★★
Next door to the tourist office, housed in the commander's residence in the old castle, is a small exhibition of Roman coins and pottery and a reconstruction of a traditional Algarvian kitchen. ⓐ Edificio do Castelo ⓛ Open Mon–Thurs 09.00–17.30 and Sat 10.00–14.00

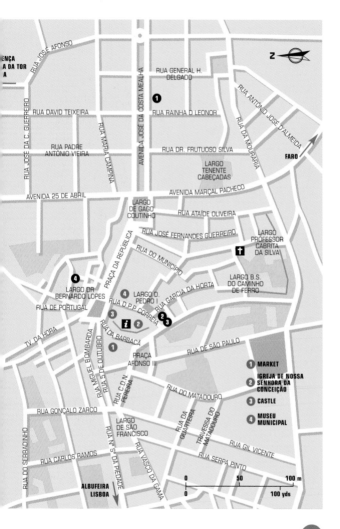

RUA JOSÉ AFONSO
ENÇA
A DA TOR
A
RUA JOSÉ DA C. GUERREIRO
RUA DAVID TEIXEIRA
RUA PADRE
ANTÓNIO VIEIRA
RUA MARIA CAMPINA
RUA JOSÉ DA C. GUERREIRO
AVENIDA 25 DE ABRIL
AVENIDA JOSÉ DA COSTA MEALHA
RUA GENERAL H.
DELGADO
RUA RAINHA D. LEONOR
RUA DR. FRUTUOSO SILVA
RUA ANTÓNIO JOSÉ D'ALMEIDA
RUA DA MOURARIA
FARO
LARGO
TENENTE
CABEÇADAS
AVENIDA MARÇAL PACHECO
LARGO
DE GAGO
COUTINHO
RUA ATAÍDE OLIVEIRA
RUA JOSÉ FERNANDES GUERREIRO
LARGO
PROFESSOR
CABRITA
DA SILVA
RUA DO MUNICÍPIO
PRAÇA DA REPÚBLICA
LARGO B.S.
DO CAMINHO
DE FERRO
LARGO DR
BERNARDO LOPES
RUA DE PORTUGAL
LARGO D.
PEDRO I
RUA D.P.P. CORREIA
RUA GARCIA DA HORTA
RUA MIGUEL BOMBARDA
RUA 5 DE OUTUBRO
RUA DA BARBAÇÃ
TV. DA HORA
PRAÇA
AFONSO III
RUA DE SÃO PAULO
RUA C.D.N.
PEREIRA
RUA DO MATADOURO
RUA GONÇALO ZARCO
LARGO
DE SÃO
FRANCISCO
RUA DA
GUARTEIRA
TRAVESSA DO
MATADOURO
RUA GIL VICENTE
RUA DO SERRADINHO
RUA CARLOS RAMOS
RUA N's DA PIEDADE
RUA VASCO DA GAMA
RUA SERPA PINTO
ALBUFEIRA
LISBOA

1 MARKET
2 IGREJA DE NOSSA
SENHORA DA
CONCEIÇÃO
3 CASTLE
4 MUSEU
MUNICIPAL

0   50   100 m
0   100 yds

SHOPPING

There's a **daily market** in Loulé, in the Moorish-style building at the top of the main street, the Avenida José da Costa Mealha, but most visitors come on Saturday morning to see the colourful **gypsy market**. There's no shortage of gifts and souvenirs – everything from handbags and *esparto* (sea grass) mats to painted roosters and ceramic plates, as well as an enormous range of food, including olives, spices, cheeses and jars of local honey.

RESTAURANTS (see map on page 89)

Avenida Velha €€–€€€ ❶ Long-established, well-known Portuguese restaurant specializing in fresh fish. ⓐ Avenida José da Costa Mealha 40/Rua Rainha D. Leonor ❶ 289 41 64 74 ● Open noon–15.30 and 18.00–22.30, closed Sun

Bica Velha €€€ ❷ Highly rated Portuguese and international cooking served up in the oldest building in town. ⓐ Rua Martim Moniz 17/19 ❶ 289 46 33 76 ● Open 18.00–midnight, closed Sun ❶ Reservations recommended

A Muralha €€ ❸ Tucked under the castle walls, serving grilled meats and fish, *cataplanas* and tapas. The garden is sweet with jasmine. ⓐ Rua Martin Moniz 41 ❶ 289 41 26 25 ● Open Mon–Tues 19.00–23.00, Wed–Sat noon–15.00 and 19.00–23.00

Paralelo 38 €–€€ ❹ Plain and simple dining from a short menu in a traditional house. ⓐ Rua Sá de Miranda ❶ No telephone bookings ● Open Mon–Sat noon–15.00 and 19.00–22.00, closed Sun

Restaurante de Querença €€€ ❺ Game dishes are on offer in this village restaurant north of Loulé. ⓐ Largo da Igreja, Querença ❶ 289 42 25 40 ● Open noon–15.00 and 19.00–late, closed Wed

Food & drink

SOUPS & STARTERS

Usually made from fish or vegetables, soups make a nourishing, tasty and relatively cheap option for a first course when dining out. Try *caldo verde*, made from shredded cabbage and potatoes, often served with thin slices of sausage, or *caldeirada de peixe*, a delicious fish soup similar to a *bouillabaisse*. Alternative starters include cured ham, prawn omelette and shellfish.

BACALHAU À BRÁS

A Portuguese favourite, this consists of salt cod, shredded and fried with onions, garlic and potato.

CATAPLANA

This tasty seafood casserole takes its name from the copper vessel the food is cooked in. Apart from clams, the ingredients usually include prawns, mussels and pieces of white fish steamed in their own juices. Pork and/or spicy sausage is often added. Servings of *cataplana* are usually for a minimum of two persons.

COFFEE

The Portuguese are great coffee drinkers and there are numerous ways it can be served:

- espresso-style black coffee is *um café* or *uma bica*.
- coffee with milk is *café com leite*.
- iced coffee is *café gelado*.
- regular black coffee is *uma carioca*.
- milky coffee, served in a glass, is *um galão*.

The daily catch is landed at numerous little harbours

FRESH FISH

A typically Algarvian dish, charcoal-grilled sardines are cheap and available everywhere, always served with fresh bread and boiled potatoes. The daily catch in most resorts includes tuna, swordfish, sea bass, bream, sole and red mullet. Most types of fish are simply grilled, but tuna may be cooked in a casserole with onions and peppers.

 When ordering fish, check the price carefully – it may be calculated by weight or *preço variável* (varying according to season and availability).

MEAT DISHES

Popular with tourists, chicken *piri-piri* is an African-influenced dish in which the chicken pieces are brushed with a chilli and olive oil sauce before being grilled. Steak or pork fillets are usually served in generous portions. *Bife à Portuguesa*, sirloin steak cooked with smoked ham and potatoes in the oven, is a succulent national dish. Also look out for *fígado com arroz*, liver and rice served in a tasty sauce, and *caldeirada de cabrita*, an appetizing lamb or kid stew.

DESSERTS

Save room for one of the delicious Portuguese desserts, choosing from crème caramel, chocolate mousse, rice pudding, almond tart or *queijo de figo* (layers of dried figs, ground almonds, cinnamon and chocolate).

CHECKING THE BILL

In Portuguese restaurants, there is a small cover charge for bread and butter, which comes with olives, fish spread and cheese. If you don't want these, say so. The Portuguese equivalent of VAT (called IVA) is usually added automatically to the bill and amounts to 12 per cent of the total. Tipping is at your own discretion, but 10 per cent would be appreciated.

DRINKS
Soft drinks

Citrus fruits are plentiful in the Algarve, though freshly squeezed juice is surprisingly expensive (if you want fizzy orange or lemonade, ask the waiter for Fanta, Sprite or 7-up). The tap water is drinkable, but it is less palatable than the home-produced mineral water from Monchique.

Wine

Portugal is a major wine-producing country, and a bottle of wine with a meal won't break the bank. Most restaurants will have an acceptable *vinho da casa* (house wine). If you want red, ask for *vinho vermelho*, if white, *vinho branco*. *Vinho verde* (literally, 'green wine') is actually a youthful and slightly sparkling wine, well suited to seafood.

Wine produced locally in the Algarve (look for the Lagoa label) tends to be high in alcohol and a little on the rough side. Portugal's better vintages are grown further north. They include Dão (similar to a Burgundy) and two good-value wines from the Alentejo region, Borba and Redondo. If you're in the mood for a celebration, try the Portuguese sparkling wine, *vinho espumante*.

Beer & spirits

Sagres and Super Bock, two good-quality lagers, are the most popular Portuguese brands. Many foreign beers are available in pubs or English-style restaurants. The local firewater, *medronho*, is distilled from the fruit of the arbutus tree. *Brandymel*, made with Portuguese brandy and locally produced honey, is a sweet liqueur, like the delicious almond-based *amêndoa amarga*.

> ### PORT
> Apart from the more common ruby and tawny port varieties, you'll come across a dry white port, served chilled as a delicious aperitif. Surprisingly, the Portuguese themselves are not great port drinkers.

Menu decoder

GENERAL
água (fresca) Water (iced)
azeite Olive oil
azeitonas Olives
bica Espresso-style coffee
cerveja Beer
chá Tea
galão White coffee (served in a tall glass)
gelo Ice
manteiga Butter
pão Bread
pimenta Pepper
prato de dia Dish of the day
queijo Cheese
sal Salt
vinagre Vinegar
vinho (branco/vermelho) Wine (white/red)
vinho de mesa/vinho de casa Table wine/house wine

TYPICAL PORTUGUESE DISHES
bacalhau Salt cod, cooked numerous ways, often with olives, garlic, onions and hard-boiled egg
bife de cebolada Steak braised in wine and onions
caldeirada Fish soup with onions and potatoes
caldo verde Soup of mashed potato and finely shredded cabbage
cozida portuguesa A rich casserole of beef, pork, sausages, rice and vegetables
sopa de grão Chickpea, tomato and onion soup
sopa de marisco Seafood soup

 Grilled sardines are cheap and available anywhere

MENU ITEMS & COOKING TERMS

On Portuguese menus, the dishes are often described very simply, with the main ingredient and the cooking method, as in *coelho assado* (roast rabbit). Here is a list of the most common ingredients and cooking methods.

alho Garlic
almôndegas Meatballs
ameijoas Clams
arroz Rice
assado Roast
atum Tuna
besugo Bream
bife (also **vaca**) Beef
bolo Cake
borrego Lamb
caracóis Snails
cavala Mackerel
cebola Onions
chouriço Spicy sausage
coelho Rabbit
costeletas Chops
cozido Boiled
robalo Sea bass
estufado Stewed
favas Broad beans
feijóes Beans
frango Chicken

fumado Smoked
gambas Prawns
gelado Ice cream
grelhado Grilled
guisado Stewed
lagostins Lobster
linguado Sole
lulas Squid
mariscos Shellfish
molho Sauce
nas brasas Braised
no forno Baked
peixe Fish
pescada Hake
pescadhina Whiting
polvos Octopus
porco Pork
presunto Cured ham
salsichão Salami
sobremesa Dessert
truta Trout
vitela Veal

Shopping

MARKETS

Every town of any size in the Algarve has a permanent covered market
where local people shop (in preference to the supermarket) for
inexpensive fruit, vegetables and fish. Larger markets also have stalls
selling bread, cured ham and local cheeses. Street markets are colourful
affairs and you may pick up some bargains – ceramics, wicker baskets,
lacework, linen, even old liquor stills. If you don't like the price, it's
acceptable to barter.

Market days at a glance

This listing shows which day or days of the month you will find markets
in towns along the Algarve coast.

- Albufeira – 1st and 3rd Tues
- Almancil – 1st and 4th Sun
- Tavira – 1st Sat
- Portimão – 1st Mon
- Alvor – 2nd Tues
- Quarteira – Every Wed
- Faro – 1st Fri and Sun
- Sagres – 1st Fri
- Lagos – 1st Sat
- Silves – 3rd Mon
- Loulé – Every Sat

🔺 *Pottery is a popular choice of souvenir*

BASKETRY

Basket weavers still work out of doors in the summer months. One popular spot to catch them practising their skills is on the EN 125 near Boliqueime (for Loulé).

CERAMICS, TILES & POTTERY

Among the most popular items are painted *gallos* (cockerels), inspired by a Portuguese folk tale. You'll also find miniature chimneys and brightly coloured jars and vases. *Azulejo* tiles – of the kind found in churches and other historic buildings – are only expensive if genuinely old. They are sold singly or in sets.

The best-known potteries in the Algarve are at Porches, 3 km (1.8 miles) east of Lagoa, where the speciality is floral-patterned *majolica*. Visit **Artesanato Reis** (🕓 Open Mon–Sat 09.00–20.00 in summer) in Porches, where you can see the craftsmen hand-painting flowers, birds, fish and other motifs.

Other pottery outlets are:

- **Artesanato Regional Casa Matias** Traditional pottery. 🅐 Mercado Municipal, Tavira 🕓 Closed Sun
- **Casa Algarve** Sells locally produced pottery, old and new. 🅐 EN 125, Alqueives, Porches
- **Domingos de Jesus Filipe** Traditional earthenware. 🅐 EN 125, Penina, Portimão
- **Infante Don Henrique** Earthenware pottery. 🅐 Rua Candido dos Reis, Albufeira
- **Olaria Algarve** Watch the craftsmen at work at this Porches outlet. 🅐 EN 124, Alqueives, Porches 🕓 Open Mon–Fri all day and Sat mornings

COPPER & BRONZE

Bowls, trays, scales, small stills and lamps are often made locally. The **Caldeiraria Louletana** (Rua da Barbacã, Loulé) is a workshop specializing in handmade brass and copperware.

CORK

Portugal is the world's largest exporter, and is famed for its cork products, ranging from placemats to whole sculptures. **O Poço**, Estrada da Foia, Monchique, sells a variety of cork items.

HANDICRAFTS

Throughout the Algarve, shops specializing in *artesanato* sell products, such as baskets, cork mats, lace tablecloths, woollen shawls, handmade rugs, brightly painted earthenware jars, copper lamps, confectionery, cockerels and *caravelles* (traditional sailing vessels made from wood).

General arts and crafts outlets:

- **Alexandre Herculano** ⓐ Monchique ⓛ Open daily
- **Aquário** ⓐ Praça da República, Portimão ⓛ Open daily
- **Arisol** ⓐ Alporchinhos, Porches ⓛ Closed Sun
- **Bazar Tânger** ⓐ Rua José Pires Padinha, Tavira ⓛ Closed Sun
- **Casa & Etc** ⓐ Rua 5 de Outubro, Albufeira ⓛ Open Mon–Fri 10.00–13.00 and 15.00–19.00
- **Casa da Praça** Wide range of handicrafts at reasonable prices. ⓐ Praça
- **Centro de Artesanato** Rugs, ceramics, straw dolls, cork placemats, palm-leaf items, lace shawls, caravelles. ⓐ Loulé ⓛ Open daily
- **Estabelecimentos Sol Dourado** ⓐ Rua Dr. Teófilo Braga, Vila Real de Santo António ⓛ Open Mon–Fri and Sat mornings
- **João Calado Earthenware** Cast iron, pottery, glazed tiles, cork and sconces. ⓐ N124, Torre, Lagos ⓛ Open daily
- **Porta da Moura** ⓐ Rua do Repouso, Faro ⓛ Open 10.00–20.00
- **Al Quatro** ⓐ Estrada de Vale do Lobo, Almancil ⓛ Open Mon–Fri 10.00–13.00 and 14.00–19.00

JEWELLERY, GOLD & SILVERWARE

Portuguese craftsmen are famous for filigree – fine threads of gold or silver delicately interwoven to produce brooches and pendants, resembling birds, flowers or cockerels. *Marcasite*, a grey-black metallic mineral, was used in Moorish jewellery and is inexpensive.

For original jewellery:
- **Allerbon** ❸ Marina, Vilamoura
- **Ingrid Serrão** ❸ Rua Direita, Portimão
- **Mogodor** ❸ Rua Gil Eanes, Lagos
- **Starte** ❸ Rua Guilherme Gomes Fernandes, Tavira

LEATHERWARE

Handbags, belts (often ornamented), wallets, purses, shoes and boots are all excellent value in Portugal, and generally of excellent quality. In Rua da Barbacã, in Loulé, you can shop for leather belts and other items; at the same time you can watch the local artisans at work, making saddles and harnesses.

MUSIC

Take home a recording of *fado* music (see page 8) as a memento of your visit. Artists to look out for include Amalia Rodrigues, Carlos do Carmo and Madredeus.

WINES & SPIRITS

Any large supermarket will have a large selection of wines and spirits. The best Algarvian wines carry the Lagoa label. Also look out for Borba, Redondo, Dão, the light wine known as *vinho verde* and quality wines from the Douro region. Port is widely available, either well-known British brands like Croft and Cockburn or Portuguese labels, including Ferreira. Wine shops also stock varieties of *medronho* (arbutus berry liqueur). Alternatively, take home some of the delicious sweet liqueur made from almonds, known as *amêndoa amarga*, or *brandymel*, Portuguese brandy blended with honey.

For any last-minute purchases before you head home, Faro airport's departure lounge has a shopping arcade. Here you can snap up handicrafts, drinks, tobacco, perfumes, regional sweets, cheeses, coffee, tea, delicatessen products, cameras, leather goods, books, stationery and CDs. ● Open 07.00–midnight

---

🔺 *An animal display at Zoomarine*

Kids

The beautifully clean beaches of the Algarve are ideally suited to young families. You can rent pedalos at most resorts. In particular, the lakes at Quinta do Lago make a very safe environment for pedalos, rowing boats, canoes, etc. There is even a children's playground here.

Conditions at Praia da Rocha and Lagos are ideal for children learning to windsurf. **The Windsurf Centre** at Meia Praia, Lagos, runs 'Kids Days' (age 9–16 years only) on Mondays and Fridays (10.30–16.00 hours) from June to September. The programme includes windsurfing lessons, volleyball, beach games and lunch – all under the watchful eye of a lifeguard.

BOAT TRIPS

Day excursions on the water leave from most resorts. Boats explore the grottoes, as well as offering opportunities for swimming, diving and snorkelling. While older children will relish the adventure, be aware that younger children may get bored. It may also be a good idea to take a boat trip on your second week, when the children have acclimatized a little to the sun and heat.

FAMILY RESTAURANTS

Most restaurants in the Algarve welcome children. Some even have high-chairs and children's choices on the menu.

KRAZY WORLD

Inland from Albufeira, this fun park, set in scenic surroundings, is well worth the half-hour trip. The attractions include crazy golf, a mini-zoo, crocodile shows, swimming pools, a Quad circuit and pedalos on the lake, plus bar, pizzeria and souvenir shop. ⓔ Algoz ⓘ 282 57 41 34 ⓦ www.krazy-world.com ⓛ Open 10.00–19.30 (May–Sept); until 18.00 (Oct–April)

PICNICS

Picnics are worth considering if you're planning a drive, a day out in the countryside or want to avoid pricey snack bars at tourist sites. There are fully stocked supermarkets in all Portuguese resorts, but remember that most shops close for lunch (usually 13.00–15.00 hours). The local market is a much more interesting place to shop – here you will find the freshest fruit and vegetables (especially oranges, peaches and figs), as well as assorted local breads, sausages, cheeses and hams.

WATER PARKS

Ideal for children of all ages (and adults too!), it is possible to spend a whole day in one of the Algarve's water parks. The biggest and best is **Slide and Splash**. **Atlantic Park** may be a quieter day for young families. Each has a number of amazingly convoluted slides, as well as junior pools, snack bars and other amenities. Fully qualified lifeguards are always on hand. Private buses take customers to and from the resorts.

- **Slide and Splash** 🅐 EN 125, Vale de Deus, Estombar, near Armação de Pêra (see page 32)
- **Atlantic Park** 🅐 EN 125, Quatro Estrados, near Quarteira (see page 44)
- **The Big One** 🅐 EN 125, Alcantarilha (see page 29)

ZOOMARINE

This spectacular attraction features dolphin, sea-lion and seal shows. Other amenities include aquariums, swimming pools, a cinema and a funfair. 🅐 On the EN125 at Guia, near Albufeira 🅣 289 56 03 00 🅦 www.zoomarine.com

🔺 *Family water fun at Algarve's water parks*

Sports & activities

BIRDWATCHING
Local birdwatching trips can be organized through the tourist offices in Portimão and Lagos (see page 12 for details).

CYCLING
Bicycles and motorbikes can be rented out by the day from **Motorent** at the following main resorts:
- Armação de Péra 🕿 282 35 65 51
- Praia da Luz 🕿 282 78 89 28
- Praia da Rocha, Hotel Rocha 2 🕿 282 41 69 98
- Praia do Carvoeiro 🕿 282 35 65 51

FISHING
- **Cepemar** Big-game fishing for hammerhead shark, marlin, swordfish, *bonito* and 200 other species. 🔘 Portimão 🕿 282 42 53 41
- **Centro de Pesca da Quinta do Lago** Fishing on the salt-water lake. Prices include all fishing equipment (see the tourist office for details and bookings).

HORSE RIDING
If you fancy enjoying the scenery from horseback, the following centres offer excursions and riding lessons for all age groups, as well as refreshments and other facilities.
- **Vale Navio** 🔘 Albufeira 🕿 289 54 28 70
- **Casa Galaraz Riding Centre** 🔘 Benagil/Carvoeiro 🕿 282 65 80 55
- **Lagoa Casa** 🔘 Agrícola Solear, Porches 🕿 282 38 14 44
- **Tiffany's Riding Centre** 🔘 Lagos 🕿 282 69 73 95
- **Grande Vale de Ferro Riding** Free pick-up from Alvor, Praia da Rocha and Portimão. 🔘 Mexilhoeira 🕿 282 96 84 44
- **Centro Hípico da Penina** 🔘 Portimão 🕿 282 41 54 15
- **Quinta dos Amigos** 🕿 289 39 33 99
- **Centro Hípico** 🔘 Vilamoura 🕿 289 32 26 75

SCUBA DIVING

- **Atlantic Scuba Diving** This PADI affiliated centre offers courses for novices, expert and specialist divers. Daily equipment hire also available. ⓐ Based at Praia da Aveiro near Albufeira ⓣ 289 58 74 79
- **Sea Sport Centre** This centre is an officially licenced diving school. Regular wreck and night dives organized. ⓐ Praia da Luz ⓣ 282 78 95 38

SPORT & FITNESS CENTRES

- **Barringtons** Squash courts, gymnasium, cricket pitch with nets, snooker room, sauna and Turkish bath, indoor and outdoor swimming pools and, for golfers, putting green, pitching green, driving range and tuition option. Daily and weekly membership available. ⓐ Vale do Lobo ⓣ 289 39 66 22
- **Burgau Sports Centre** Tennis and squash courts, sauna, gymnasium, pool, table tennis, many other sports, swimming pool and children's playground. ⓐ Burgau ⓣ 282 69 73 50
- **Rock Garden** Tennis and squash courts, gymnasium, indoor and outdoor swimming pools, snooker tables, table tennis and darts. ⓐ Vilamoura ⓣ 289 32 27 40

TENNIS

Racquet hire as well as tuition are available at the following centres.
- **Burgau Sports Centre** (see above).
- **Rocha Brava Tennis Club** ⓐ Carvoeiro ⓣ 282 35 78 47
- **David Lloyd Tennis Centre** ⓐ Vale Do Lobo ⓣ 289 39 39 39
- **Rock Garden** (see above)
- **Vilasol Tennis Centre** ⓣ 289 30 05 25

WALKING

The Algarve Walkers Club Organizes local rambles. ⓣ 282 44 90 98

Festivals & events

Algarve Events is a brochure published in several languages by the regional tourist authority (available from local tourist offices, in hotels, etc) giving up-to-date listings of cultural events.

January
1–6 January Carol singing in the local villages.

February
Carnival all over the Algarve in the weekend prior to Shrove Tuesday.
Loulé Carnival The biggest and best, with bands, colourful floats and dancers. Eggs, flour and other substances are hurled about, so visitors are advised to wear protective clothing! ❶ 289 46 39 00

March
20 March Alvor holds its annual *feria* with entertainment including live music and traditional *fado* performances.

April
Throughout the Algarve there are religious processions in the lead up to Easter, especially on Palm Sunday and Good Friday.

May
1 May The May Day folk festival involves traditional singing and folk dancing – celebrated in Alcoutim, Albufeira, Alte, Monchique.
International Film Festival ❶ 289 80 04 00

June
International Music Festival The biggest event of its kind in the Algarve, with performances by world-famous artists. ❶ 289 80 04 00
Tavira 'Saints Festivities' Dancing, processions and street decoration.
❶ 281 32 25 11

July

Tavira Jazz Festival International and local musicians. ☎ 281 32 25 11
Silves Beer Festival Local Portuguese beers, with tastings, in the grounds of the castle, plus brass band concerts and folk dancing. ☎ 282 44 22 55
Feira do Carmo Handicraft festival in Faro.
Faro Motorbike Festival Bike convention and rock music. ☎ 289 80 36 04

August

Lagoa 'Fatacil' country fair Handicrafts, tourism, agriculture, commerce and local industry, with live bands, craft exhibitions, food and wine tasting, shows, exhibitions and competitions. ☎ 289 80 04 00
Folk dancing Shows and concerts of *fado*, folk and classical music are held in the Tavira gardens all through the summer. ☎ 281 32 25 11
11 August Cabanas Fish Festival with market, dancing and *fado* music.
29 August Banho de 29 in Lagos – fireworks and live music on the local beaches. ☎ 082 76 30 31

September

National Folklore Festival A showcase for traditional Portuguese folk music and dancing, with groups performing from all over the country. Various venues, culminating in the final competition, held on the beach at Praia da Rocha. ☎ 289 80 04 00
Portimão International Photographic Exhibition ☎ 282 41 91 31
Lagoa Wine Festival Tastings to promote the local varieties and vintages.
Monte Gordo 'Nossa Senhora das Dores' annual fair With games, side shows, folk concerts and other musical entertainment. After Monte Gordo the fair moves on to Tavira. ☎ 281 32 25 11

October

Choirs Festival Concerts from all over the Algarve. ☎ 289 80 04 00
Monchique Country Fair Exhibition of local handicrafts

December

8 December Ceremonial blessing of the crib in many churches.

⬤ *The Algarve's sandy beaches stretch for miles*

Preparing to go

GETTING THERE

The cheapest way to get to the Algarve is to book a package holiday with one of the leading tour operators. Operators specializing in the Algarve offer flight-only deals or combined flight-and-accommodation packages at prices that are hard to beat by booking direct. If your travelling times are flexible, and if you can avoid the school holidays, you can find some very cheap last-minute deals using websites. You should also check the travel supplements of weekend newspapers, such as *The Sunday Times* or *The Sunday Telegraph*. They often carry advertisements for inexpensive flights, as well as classified listings for privately owned villas and apartments to rent in the Algarve.

Charter flights can be subject to long delays, so if time is critical, you might be better off paying more to travel by scheduled flight. The Portuguese national carrier, **TAP**, offers daily flights to the Algarve, operating from Heathrow. Some flights are direct, while others involve a change in Lisbon. TAP's UK office ❸ Gillingham House, 38–44 Gillingham Street, London SW1V 1HU ❶ 0845 601 0932. **British Airways** also offer charter flights (❶ 0345 222111 Ⓦ www.british-airways.com), as does the no-frills airline Easyjet (Ⓦ www.easyjet.com); and Ryan Air flights from Dublin have regular connections from Bournemouth.

BEFORE YOU LEAVE

Holidays should be about fun and relaxation, so avoid last-minute panics and stress by making your preparations well in advance.

It is not necessary to have inoculations to travel in Europe, but you should make sure you and your family are up to date with the basics, such as tetanus. It is a good idea to pack a small first-aid kit to carry with you, containing plasters, antiseptic cream, travel-sickness pills, insect repellent, bite relief cream, antihistamine tablets, painkillers and remedies for upset stomachs.

Sun lotion can be more expensive in the Algarve than in the UK, so it is worth taking a good supply of high-factor lotions. If you are taking prescription medicines, ensure that you take enough for the duration of your visit – you may find it impossible to obtain the same medicines in the Algarve. It is also worth having a dental check-up before you go.

DOCUMENTS

The most important documents you will need are your tickets and your passport. Check well in advance that your passport is up to date and has at least three months left to run (six months is even better). All children, including newborn babies, need their own passport now, unless they are already included on the passport of the person they are travelling with. It generally takes at least a month to process a passport renewal. This can be longer in the run-up to the summer months. For the latest information on how to renew your passport and the processing times call the **Passport Agency** ❶ 0870 521 0410 Ⓦ www.ukpa.gov.uk.

You should check the details of your travel tickets well before your departure, ensuring that the timings and dates are correct.

If you are thinking of hiring a car while you are away, you, and any other drivers wishing to use the car, will need to have your driving licences with you.

MONEY

You will need some currency before you go (Portugal uses the euro), especially if your flight gets you to your destination at the weekend or late in the day after the banks have closed. Traveller's cheques are a safe way to carry money, because the money will be refunded if the cheques are lost or stolen, however they can be difficult to cash in Portugal. ATMs are also safe and give a good exchange rate. To buy traveller's cheques or exchange money at a bank you may need to give up to a week's notice, depending on the quantity of euros you require. You can also exchange money at the airport before you depart.

If you plan to use credit, charge or debit cards while you are away, call your bank or card company before you leave to let them know where you are going. Otherwise you may find your card abruptly stopped while you are away. You can also check that your cards are up to date – you do not want them to expire mid-holiday – and that your credit limit is sufficient for those holiday purchases. Don't forget, too, to check your PIN numbers in case you haven't used them for a while – you may want to draw money from cash dispensers while you are away.

INSURANCE

Check that your policy covers you adequately for loss of possessions and valuables, for activities you might want to try – such as scuba diving, horse riding or water sports – and for emergency medical and dental treatment, including flights home if required. After January 2006, a new EHIC card replaces the E111 form to allow UK visitors access to reduced-cost, and sometimes free state-provided medical treatment in the EEA. For further information, ring EHIC enquiries line: ☎ 0845 605 0707 or visit the Department of Health website ⓦ www.dh.gov.uk.

CLIMATE

The weather in the Algarve has attracted tourists to the region for centuries, and the climate is one of the most settled in the world. With over 3000 hours of sunshine a year, the climate is similar to that of northern Africa. Winters are generally mild, with temperatures rarely dipping below 10°C (50°F); summers are hot, often exceeding 30°C (86°F). A constant feature of the annual climate is the sea breeze, refreshing in summer, bracing in winter. Rainfall is low and mostly falls in October and November, and February and March.

CLOTHING

It is always worth bringing a light sweater, though for much of the year you will probably be comfortable in shorts and a T-shirt. The hottest period is between June and September, and spring temperatures (April–May) are also fairly dependable. Something light to keep out the wind is advisable in all but the hottest months.

As a haven for the international holidaymaker, the general level of dress in the Algarve is very casual. The only places you might need something smarter is in a restaurant in the evening.

SECURITY

Take precautions to avoid your home being burgled while you are away.

- Cancel milk, newspapers and other regular deliveries.
- Let the postman know where to leave parcels and bulky mail that will not go through your letterbox – ideally with a neighbour.
- Consider buying electrical timing devices that switch lights and radios on and off, to give the impression there is someone at home.
- Let Neighbourhood Watch representatives know you will be away so they can keep an eye on your home.
- If you have a burglar alarm, make sure it is working properly. Ensure a neighbour is able to turn the alarm off if it is accidentally activated.
- If you are leaving cars unattended, put them in a garage, if possible, and leave a key with a neighbour in case the alarm goes off.

TELEPHONING PORTUGAL

To call Portugal from the UK, dial **00** followed by **351**, then the nine-digit number – there's no need to wait for a dialling tone.

During your stay

AIRPORTS

The main airport for the Algarve is at Faro, and this is one of the cheapest and most competitive routes in Europe, thanks to the sheer number of charter flights travelling between the UK and the Algarve. Even so, flights are often fully booked during the peak holiday periods, including Christmas: the Algarve is a very popular winter-sun destination.

Faro airport is several kilometres west of the city and, if you land by day from the south, you will have a stunning view of the Ria Formosa Nature Reserve, where land and sea meet in a protected zone. The airport has many of the services you would expect, including a bank, a post office, a tourist office, shops and restaurants. Faro is the capital of the Algarve region and therefore all transport services are available, including car rental.

CURRENCY

Money In line with the majority of EU member states, Portugal entered the single currency on 1 January 2002. Euro (€) note denominations are 500, 200, 100, 50, 20, 10 and 5. Coins are €1 and €2, and 1, 2, 5, 10, 20 and 50 céntimos.

Banks Open Monday to Friday 08.30–15.00. There are exchange shops (câmbios) everywhere in the Algarve. You will need to show your passport when exchanging travellers' cheques.

Credit cards These are widely accepted at garages, shops and restaurants in the major towns, but cash is preferred in more rural areas.

BEACHES

In summer, many beaches have lifeguards and a flag safety system. Other beaches may be safe for swimming, but there are unlikely to be life-saving amenities available. Bear in mind that the strong winds that develop in the hotter months can quickly change a safe beach into a not-so-safe one, and some have strong currents the further out you go. If in doubt, ask the tourist office or at your hotel.

BEACH SAFETY
Take note of the flag system that advises you of swimming conditions.
- **Green** = safe bathing and swimming for all
- **Yellow** = caution – strong swimmers only
- **Red** = danger – no swimming

CHILDREN'S ACTIVITIES

The Algarve is a great holiday destination for families. Children are cherished in Portugal and you will find they are welcome in most restaurants. There is sometimes even a separate children's menu available. Most tour operators offer a kids' club in the larger hotels, providing appropriate activities for different age groups throughout your stay. This provides them with supervision and friends away from their parents if they choose the activities on offer. A lot of hotels offer a baby-sitting service as well. In addition to this, there are a number of activities in the Algarve aimed at children (see page 102 for more details).

GETTING AROUND
Car rental and driving

Portugal has a wide range of car rental companies. All the well-known ones are to be found at the airport. Others can be contacted via your hotel or holiday representative. To rent a car in Portugal you must be over 21 years old and have held your licence for at least one year. You will need to show your driving licence and carry it with you whenever you are driving (as will any other named drivers on your rental agreement). Make sure the insurance cover is sufficient for your needs.

Driving in Portugal can be unpredictable, so take extreme care. Drivers here can be impatient when faced with a driver who is not used to the area. Many back roads are very narrow and the surfaces may be uneven. However, a lot of main roads have recently been resurfaced, and motorways are being extended for easier access to all parts of Portugal.

Rules of the road

- Always carry your driving licence, car-rental papers and passport. Police checks are infrequent, but you will be fined if you do not have the correct papers.
- Seat belts are compulsory, even for back-seat passengers. Children under 12 are not allowed in the front.
- The speed limit is 120 km/h (74 mph) on motorways, 90 km/h (56 mph) on highways, and 40–50 km/h (25–30 mph) in villages, towns and cities.
- Drink-drive and speeding laws are rigorously applied. The alcohol limit is lower than in the UK.
- The local driving can be erratic. Always drive with extreme caution.

Taxis

Taxis can be hired from railway stations, bus stations and taxi ranks. If you decide to use a taxi for a longer journey (a day trip for example), it is possible to negotiate the fare. It will help to write down your destination – many drivers speak only limited English.

Buses

Buses operate along the main EN 125 highway, linking the resorts and main villages. Stops are marked with blue and white *paragem* signs. Timetables are posted at stops. Tickets for local buses are sold on board by the driver. Enquire about passes, which are sold at bus terminals or ticket agencies. Express buses operate between the main towns. Tickets for these must be bought from a bus terminal or ticket agency before boarding. It is advisable to book in advance at the height of the season.

Trains

A railway runs from Vila Real de Santo António near the Spanish border to Lagos in the west. If you are not in a hurry, this is a good way to see inland Algarve. The trains are clean and airy, if a little basic, and very cheap. Be warned that a number of stations – Loulé, Silves and Albufeira, for example – are some distance from the town centres.

Cycles and motorbikes

Mountain bikes, cycles, scooters, mopeds and motorbikes can all be hired from various outlets in the Algarve. However, due to the number of accidents in Portugal involving motorized bikes, these are not recommended.

VISITORS WITH DISABILITIES

In general, facilities for wheelchair users are very poor in the Algarve. Many of the ramps and kerbs designed for wheelchairs will make you feel like you are mountaineering. Better facilities can be found in the international-standard hotels, where foreign travel agencies have insisted on them. The situation is slowly improving and most municipal areas will have reasonable facilities. Bus stops have been adapted to enable easier access and there are designated disabled places available on buses. Many streets are cobbled, and there are often steep hills or steps. This makes it difficult to gain access to a number of places.

HEALTH & HYGIENE

Insects Mosquitoes are attracted by light, so keep your balcony doors or windows closed when the lights are on. Inexpensive anti-mosquito machines that plug into electric sockets are a good investment, as are repellent creams and sprays.

Water Tap water in the resorts is safe to drink but has a high mineral content, so you may prefer to buy bottled water instead.

SUN PROTECTION
- Never go out without the protection of a high-factor sun cream.
- Remember to re-apply sun creams every one to two hours.
- Ensure children are protected with total sun block.
- Start off slowly and gradually increase the length of your sunbathing sessions over the holiday, as your skin adjusts.
- Avoid lying out during the hottest part of the day (noon–15.00).
- Wear a hat, as sea breezes can disguise even the strongest sun.

PERSONAL SECURITY

For your personal security, it is wise to be cautious. Portugal has a low crime rate, but, as in any country, pickpockets operate in crowded places. If possible, keep valuables in the hotel safe. If taking cash on holiday, only carry a small amount with you, in case it is lost or stolen (traveller's cheques are easier to replace). As in other places, women should not travel alone late at night, and it is advisable to keep to well-lit areas.

Should you need to report a theft or any other crime, you must go to the nearest station of the *Policia de Segurança Pública*, the national police service. The only document you may need is your passport. They will record the incident and give you a crime reference number. Trying to speak a few words of Portuguese (see page 122) will probably win you some extra enthusiasm from the other side of the desk.

If reporting the loss or theft of your passport, you will also need to get in touch with the British Consulate, who can arrange a new passport (time permitting) or issue a temporary document to get you home. It is a good idea to take photocopies of your passport before leaving home, and to keep these in a separate place from your other documents.

WHAT TO DO IN AN EMERGENCY

- Dial **112** – the operator will put you through to **police**, **fire brigade** or **ambulance**.
- Report any theft or accident to the police and your holiday representative or the hotel staff, who also keep a list of English-speaking doctors and local pharmacies.

24-hour medical assistance

- Albufeira 289 39 61 57
- Lagos 282 78 98 11
- Loulé 289 41 01 03
- Vila Real de Santo António 281 511371

First-aid posts are at the following beaches: Altura, Alvor, Armação de Pêra, Ilha da Arona, Farol, Fuseta, Manta Rota, Rocha, Sagres and Tavira. Pharmacies also deal with minor medical problems.

Police

There are three types of police service in Portugal.

Policia Municipal These are the local police in large towns who have limited powers and are governed by individual town councils. Their role is directing traffic, monitoring parking and other general business.

Policia de Segurança Pública (PSP) The national police service operates much as the British police service does, though they work mainly in large and medium-sized towns. Both these and the Policia Municipal can be recognised by their blue uniforms.

The Guarda Nacional Republicana (GNR) This militarized police service who operate throughout the national road network with their *Brigada de Trânsito* (traffic division) and in the smaller villages and rural areas throughout Portugal. They can be recognised by their green uniforms.

Consulate

In most situations your first port of call should be local sources of information or help. If all else fails, contact the **British Consulate** ⓐ Largo Francisco A. Maurício Nº7–1º, Portimão ⓣ 282 41 78 00

MEDIA

There are a few English newspapers published in Portugal, including the *APN* (Anglo-Portuguese News) and *The News*, plus the *Algarve Gazette* and the *Algarve News*. They provide stories about national news and events within the English communities. They also give a timetable of cinema showings and theatre events. Many UK newspapers are available in Portugal. You can often buy them on the day of issue, due to the fact that they are printed simultaneously in Spain and the UK.

POST OFFICES

Post offices are known as *correios* and are open on weekdays between 08.30 and 18.30 hours. There are often bigger post offices in the larger towns, which may also open on Saturday mornings. Second-class post is posted in the red post boxes. First-class post is known as *correio azul* (blue post) and therefore goes in the blue post boxes. You will sometimes see international post boxes as well. There are generally two collections a day – one at 13.00 and one at 18.00 hours.

OPENING HOURS

Shops Normally open 09.00–19.00 with a break for lunch between noon and 15.00 hours. New shopping centres often have longer hours, 10.00–23.00, including Sundays, with no lunch break.

Museums Usually open 10.00–17.00, again with a break for lunch. Many museums are closed on Mondays as well as public holidays.

Banks Open 08.30–15.00, Monday to Friday.

Pharmacies Open from 09.00–19.00, with a break for lunch. A sign in the window will tell you which pharmacy is open until 22.00 hours and where the all-night pharmacy is.

ELECTRICITY

Portugal uses the standard round-pin European plug. It is a 220-volt system as opposed to the 240-volt UK system. Before you buy electrical appliances to take home, always check they will work in the UK.

TELEPHONES

Public telephones in Portugal are either coin or card operated. Card-operated phones take credit cards or telephone cards, which can be purchased in many *tabacarias* (newsagents/cigarette shops) or from vending machines in some of the larger post offices.

If you wish to use your mobile phone on holiday, check with your phone company before you leave to find out if your mobile will work in Portugal and how much the calls will cost you.

PHONING HOME

To call an overseas number, dial **00** followed by the country code (UK = **44**). Then dial the area code (minus the initial 0) and the number you want

TIME DIFFERENCES

Portugal is the only other European country on Greenwich Mean Time. Some years ago, Portugal tried to synchronize with Spanish time, but being so westerly, the daylight hours just didn't suit them.

TIPPING

It is customary, but not essential, to tip in Portugal. A tip of 10 per cent is gratefully received in restaurants and cafés. You may wish to tip helpful taxi drivers or hotel staff, too.

WEIGHTS & MEASURES

Imperial to metric

1 inch = 2.54 centimetres
1 foot = 30.5 centimetres
1 mile = 1.61 kilometres
1 ounce = 28.35 grams
1 pound = 0.45 kilograms
1 pint = 0.56 litres
1 gallon = 4.55 litres

Metric to imperial

1 centimetre = 0.39 inches
1 metre = 3 feet, 3 inches
1 kilometre = 0.62 miles
1 gram = 0.04 ounces
1 kilogram = 2.21 pounds
1 litre = 1.76 pints

RELIGION

Portugal is predominantly Roman Catholic, with church services held most evenings and every Sunday. Many saints' days are celebrated, often as public holidays, so some tourist sights will be closed and churches may have extra services. However, you may be lucky enough to join in the celebrations at a festival to commemorate a saint's day. These are usually joyous events, often with fireworks.

CUSTOMS

The Portuguese are a gentle and friendly people. A simple good morning *(bom dia)* or good afternoon *(boa tarde)* will delight them. The sense of the family is very strong; the early evening walkabout and family church-going are still popular. Unlike much of Portugal, the Algarvians take a Spanish-style siesta, so you may find places closed in the afternoon.

THE LANGUAGE

Portuguese people respond very warmly to visitors who attempt to speak a little of their language. Here are some words to help you make a start.

ENGLISH	PORTUGUESE (pronunciation)
General vocabulary	
yes	*sím* (seengh)
no	*não* (naw)
thank you	*obrigado* (obriGAHdoo male speaking)/ *obrigada* (obriGAHdah female speaking)
hello	*olá* (ohLAH)
goodbye	*adeus* (ahDAYoosh)
good morning	*bom dia* (bom DEEah)
good afternoon	*boa tarde* (BOHah tard)
good evening/night	*boa noite* (BOHah noyt)
sorry	*desculpe* (deshCOOLpuh)
may I pass?	*com licença?* (com leeSENsah?)
Don't mention it	*De nada* (de NARdah)
Help!	*Socorro!* (sohCOHroo!)
How much?	*Quanto custa?* (KWANtoo KOOshtah?)
toilets	*sanitários* (sanyTAHreeoosh)/ *casa de banho* (KAHza de BAHNyoo)
gents/ladies	*homens* (OHmaynsh)/ *senhoras* (senYHORersh)
open	*aberto* (uhBERtoo)
closed	*fechado* (feshAHdo)
beach	*praia* (PRAeeya)
church	*igreja* (eeGRAYjuh)
museum	*museu* (mooSAYoo)
chemist	*famàcia* (farmAHseeya)
Do you sell ...?	*Vendem ...?* (VENdeyn?)
Do you speak English?	*Fala inglès?* (FAluh eenGLESH?)
I don't understand...	*Não compreendo* (naw compreeENdoo)...
I understand...	*compreendo* (compreeENdoo)...
Useful words and phrases	
room	*quarto* (KWARtoo)
single/double	*um quarto simples* (oom KWARtoo SEEMplesh)/*quarto duplo* (KWARtoo DOOploo)

ENGLISH	**PORTUGUESE** (pronunciation)
Useful words and phrases	
one/two nights	*uma noite* (ooma noyt)/ *duas noites* (DOOahsh NOYtash)
How much per night?	*Quanto custa por noite?* (KWANtoo KOOSHtah poor noyt?)
reservation	*reserva* (reeSAIRvah)
with bath/shower	*com banho* (com BANyoo)/ *chuveiro* (shooVEHYroo)
Is breakfast included?	*O pequeno almoço está incluido* (oo peeKENoo alMOHsoo shtah inklooEEdoo?)
exchange bureau	*câmbio* (KAMbeeoo)
post office	*correio* (kooRAYoo)
postage stamps	*selos* (SELLoosh)
receipt	*recibo* (rehSEEboo)
credit card	*cartão de credito* (karTAWH de KREdeetoo)
traveller's cheque	*cheque de viagem* (shehk de veeAHjayng)
restaurant	*restaurante* (restawRANT)
table	*mesa* (MAYsah)
non-smoking area	*uma área de não fumadores* (OOmah AHrayah de naw foomahDOOResh)
menu	*ementa* (eeMENtah)
tourist menu	*ementa turistica* (eeMENtah tooRISTeekah)
children's menu	*ementa para crianças* (eeMENtah PAHrah creeANsash)
vegetarian dishes	*pratos vegetarianos* (PRAHtoosh vejehtuhreeANosh)
wine list	*carta de vinhos* (KAHRtah de VEENyoosh)
A table for two, please.	*Uma mesa para dois, se faz favor* (OOmah MAYsah PAHrah DOHeesh, suh faj fahVOOR)
smoking/non-smoking	*fumadores* (foomahDOOResh)/ *não fumadores* (naw foomahDOOResh)
Another beer, please.	*Mais uma cerveja, se faz fovor* (maheez OOmah sehrVEYjah, suh faj fahVOOR)
Can I see the wine list, please?	*A carta dos vinhos, se faz favor?* (ah KAHRtah doosh VEENyoosh, suh faj fahVOOR?)
Can we have the bill, please?	*A conta, se faz favor?* (a CONtah, suh faj fahVOOR?)

ENGLISH	PORTUGUESE (pronunciation)
Useful words and phrases	
Where is the bathroom, please?	*Onde e a casa de banho, se faz favor?* (ONdee eh ah KAHza de BAHNyoo, suh faj fahVOOR?)
airport	*aeroporto* (ayrowPORtoo)
bus	*autocarro* (ortoeKAHroo)
station	*estação de autocarros* (estahSAOO dee ortoeKAHroosh)
stop	*paragem* (pahRAjeyn)
ticket office	*bilheteira* (beelyehTEYrah)
a ticket to ...	*um bilhete para ...* (oom beeLYET PAHrah)
first/second class ticket	*bilhete de primeira classe* (beeLYET duh preeMAYruh klas)/*segunda classe* (suhGOONduh klas)
timetable	*horário* (orARReeoo)
taxi rank	*ponto de táxi* (PONto duh TAKsee)
petrol	*gasolina* (gazohLEEnah)
Fill the tank, please.	*Encha o depósito, por favor* (ENshuhoduhPOZitoo, poor fuhVOOR)
car park	*parque de estacionamento* (PARkuh di staseeonahMENtoo)
left/right	*esquerdo/direito* (eshKERdoo/deeRAYtoo)
I'd like to send this to England.	*Queria mandar isto para Inglaterra.* (keyREEah manDAR EEshtoo PAHrah eengluhTEHrah)
How much is a stamp for England?	*Quanto custa um selo para mandar para Inglaterra?* (KWANtoo KOOSHtah oom SELLoo PAHrah manDAR PAHrah eengluhTEHrah)
When will it be ready?	*Quando estará pronto?* (KWANdoo shtuhRAH PRONtoo?)
Monday	*Segunda-feira* (suhGOONduhFEYruh)
Tuesday	*Terça-feira* (TERsaFEYruh)
Wednesday	*Quarta-feira* (KWARtuhFEYruh)
Thursday	*Quinta-feira* (KEENtuhFEYruh)
Friday	*Sexta-feira* (SESHtuhFEYruh)
Saturday	*Sábado* (SAbuhdoo)
Sunday	*Domingo* (dooMINgoo)
today	*hoje* (ohj)
tomorrow	*amanhã* (ahmanYAH)
yesterday	*ontem* (ONtayn)

ACKNOWLEDGEMENTS

We would like to thank all the photographers, picture libraries and organisations for the loan of the photographs reproduced in this book, to whom copyright in the photograph belongs:
Brian and Eileen Anderson (pages 57);
JupiterImages Corporation (pages 97, 107, 125);
Pictures Colour Library Ltd (pages 91);
Rogers Associates (pages 87, 59);
Thomas Cook Tour Operations Ltd (pages 9, 11, 13, 16, 21, 1, 24, 30, 32, 40, 45, 48, 60, 77, 92, 97, 98, 102, 104, 110, 5)

We would also like to thank the following for their contribution to this series:
John Woodcock (map and symbols artwork);
Becky Alexander, Patricia Baker, Sophie Bevan, Judith Chamberlain-Webber, Nicky Gyopari, Stephanie Horner, Krystyna Mayer, Robin Pridy (editorial support);
Christine Engert, Suzie Johanson, Richard Lloyd, Richard Peters, Alistair Plumb, Jane Prior, Barbara Theisen, Ginny Zeal, Barbara Zuñiga (Design support)

Send your thoughts to
books@thomascook.com

- Found a beach bar, peaceful stretch of sand or must-see sight that we don't feature?

- Like to tip us off about any information that needs a little updating?

- Want to tell us what you love about this handy, little guidebook and more importantly how we can make it even handier?

Then here's your chance to tell all! Send us ideas, discoveries and recommendations today and then look out for your valuable input in the next edition of this title. And, as an extra 'thank you' from Thomas Cook Publishing, you'll be automatically entered into our exciting monthly prize draw.

Email to the above address or write to:
HotSpots Project Editor, Thomas Cook Publishing, PO Box 227, Unit 15/16, Coningsby Road, Peterborough PE3 8SB, UK.